No
Crowns
in the
Castle

No Crowns in the Castle

Building a Strong Relationship and a Harmonious Life

FANTASIA AND KENDALL TAYLOR

WITH HILARY BEARD

New York • Nashville

Worthy
Hachette Book Group
1290 Avenue of the Americas, New York, NY 10104
worthypublishing.com
twitter.com/worthypub

First Edition: April 2022

Worthy is a division of Hachette Book Group, Inc. The Worthy name and logo are trademarks of Hachette Book Group, Inc.

The publisher is not responsible for websites (or their content) that are not owned by the publisher.

The Hachette Speakers Bureau provides a wide range of authors for speaking events. To find out more, go to www.hachettespeakersbureau.com or call (866) 376-6591.

Unless otherwise noted, Scripture quotations are taken from the Holy Bible, New International Version®. Copyright © 1973, 1978, 1984, 2011 by Biblica, Inc.™ Used by permission of Zondervan. All rights reserved worldwide. www.zondervan.com. The "NIV" and "New International Version" are trademarks registered in the United States Patent and Trademark Office by Biblica, Inc.™ Scriptures marked KJV are from the King James Version of the Holy Bible.

Print book interior design by Bart Dawson.

Library of Congress Cataloging-in-Publication Data
Names: Taylor, Fantasia Barrino, author. | Taylor, Kendall, 1941- author. | Beard, Hilary, author.
Title: No crowns in the castle : building a strong relationship and a harmonious life / Kendall and Fantasia Taylor with Hilary Beard.
Description: First edition. | Nashville : Worthy, [2022] | Summary: "Leave
  your crown at the door. Fantasia Barrino Taylor-American Idol, Grammy-winning vocalist, and chart-topping singer-and her husband businessman Kendall Taylor were both successful and living in their purpose when they met and married three weeks later. Their marriage has had its ups and downs, but the one thing that has sustained them through all of it is the practice of taking off their crowns-the accolades, their egos, the things the world tells you matter-and serving each other within the home. It doesn't matter who you are in the world-you need to humble yourself and serve your partner in order to put your marriage, your family, and your faith first. Seven years later, after facing a host of real-world challenges-from marital stress to professional and financial pressures, to their high-risk pregnancy and the premature birth of their daughter-Fantasia and Kendall's marriage has become a beacon of hope and love as they have opened up about their lives in their weekly 'Taylor Talks' broadcast. Now, in their first book together, Fantasia and Kendall dish about their shared experiences and struggles, opening up about the challenges and triumphs they've faced together and how they have come out stronger for them. They also share stories about how they've made their relationship work against all odds and why they try to always treat each other like royalty. In their trademark no-nonsense, real-talk style, they discuss topics that affect all relationships, including the importance of submitting to one another, handling conflict, clearing the lines of communication, keeping the romance alive, navigating the challenges of blended family, and how to maintain healthy relationships when you haven't seen them modeled before. Insightful, wise, and grounded in faith, Fantasia and Kendall's story offers hope and encouragement and gives straight-up advice about making your relationships last"— Provided by publisher.
Identifiers: LCCN 2021047745 | ISBN 9781546012634 (hardcover) | ISBN 9781546012627 (ebook)
Subjects: LCSH: Marriage—Religious aspects—Christianity. | Pride and vanity—Religious aspects—Christianity. | Self—Religious aspects—Christianity.
Classification: LCC BV835 .T39 2022 | DDC 248.8/44—dc23/eng/20211206
LC record available at https://lccn.loc.gov/2021047745

ISBNs: 978-1-5460-1263-4 (hardcover), 978-1-5460-0270-3 (signed edition), 978-1-5460-0262-8 (Barnes & Noble signed edition), 978-1-5460-1262-7 (ebook)

Printed in the United States of America
LSC-C
Printing 1, 2022

This book is dedicated to our mothers,
Diane Barber and Donna Bouie.
Through their countless and unselfish examples of sacrifice,
these incredible women showed us the pure love
that became the foundation upon which we've built
an even greater understanding.

Contents

Introduction

FANTASIA

I was promoting my most recent album, *Sketchbook*, at the end of 2019, when I was invited onto the morning radio show *The Breakfast Club*. I was excited to talk about the single "PTSD." *Sketchbook* is very different from my previous albums. My past songs hadn't been exactly positive about men. I had been in bad relationships, and I wrote songs that reflected that truth. One of my most popular albums was called *Free Yourself*, and it was written to empower women to walk away from bad relationships:

If you don't want me then don't talk to me
Go ahead and free yourself.

I had so many broken people following me, and this song healed a lot of hearts.

But *Sketchbook* was a different kind of album for me because I'm in a very different kind of relationship now. As I sit down to write this book, I have been married for almost seven years. When I first met Kendall, my husband, I saw in him everything I had been asking God for. And the longer I'm with him, the more I know why God sent him to me. I'm also in a different relationship with my music. *Sketchbook* is the first album I produced independently. That means I can make the kind of music I want. No more people telling me what I can and cannot do. That made me stupid excited about promoting it—even more than I'd usually be.

I'd never been on *Breakfast Club* before. Real talk, I wasn't exactly looking forward to going on. I thank God for my gift and my ministry, but I don't exactly love the music industry. After winning *American Idol* at age nineteen, I had been performing for fifteen years straight and everyone had been making money but me. My contract was structured so other people were making money on songwriting royalties and album sales; if I wanted to get paid, I had to perform. That meant I'd had to function like a workaholic. I'd spent too much time away from my children and had missed so many special moments. I'd blown out both my knees. By the fall of 2019 I was bone-tired and needed to rest.

I was also afraid that I'd make a mistake in the interview and end up on *MediaTakeOut* or one of the other gossip publications or websites and get roasted. So, I was nervous about going on-air.

But I love this album, and they promised they'd play my music, so I figured I'd take a chance and go. I was ready to defend myself and my art. Music is my ministry.

KENDALL

I recall well the conversation that I had with my Queen, when she was first asked to consider doing the *Breakfast Club* interview. The hesitancy that my wife expressed was natural and to be expected. She's a true soul singer with a gentle spirit and didn't necessarily fit the model of a typical *B. Club* guest, which has more of a "shock jock" format. Normally, doing the *Breakfast Club* interview wouldn't make sense, but in this case it did because "PTSD," the single being promoted, had crossover potential; the benefit of presenting it to the hip-hop audience was undeniable. I personally watch many *Breakfast Club* interviews and have my finger on the pulse of how they handle a variety of guests. I felt comfortable that my Queen would be treated with care and respect by the hosts and so I encouraged her to step outside of her comfort zone and to be open to doing the interview.

FANTASIA

The hosts, DJ Envy and Angela Yee, started off by asking me about the music. They mentioned the fact that my messages about relationships on this album were positive and asked what made me shift my tone.

I explained that because I'm married, I'm not really singing about the same things that I used to. Through sharing my gift, my ministry, in front of so many audiences, I've also witnessed music's power, I said, and I knew that music can be a healer, but it can also contribute to a spirit of discord. When people listen to music about men and women fighting, they are more likely to end up at war in their relationships. I had found love and wanted other people to experience it too. I wanted to make music that brings people together.

"Do you think that's the kind of stuff your audience wants to hear?" Angela asked me.

"Are you in a relationship?" I replied.

"No, I want to be in one and I'm looking."

"If you keep listening to songs like 'Free Yourself' and 'Bittersweet,' you'll never find that relationship. You'll never find that one," I told her.

I knew a forward statement like that could be taken out of context, but I was up to the challenge of the show, so I shared anyway.

While we were chopping it up, DJ Envy told me he had been married for eighteen years and he and his wife had been together for twenty-five.

"What's the key?" I asked him, excited to hear that they'd stayed together so long. He talked about the importance of communication and forgiveness. He had opened the door for me to take it a little further and to get into a spiritual conversation, so I went for it.

"What about prayer?"

"Every day."

"Together?"

"Every morning I wake my wife up before I leave," he said, then went on to describe their prayers.

"That's what's up!" I told him. "I salute you. We need more men to stand up and lead the way. Most women are trying to be the leader; that's why you can't find a man," I said. "You can't be the king in the house. Fall back and be the queen and let your man lead the way."

When host Angela Yee asked what I meant, I said that a generational curse has undermined many families and caused too many women to have to handle everything all the time—work, pay the bills, raise the kids alone, make all the decisions, stand up and be strong, and act like a man. I described a vision of men and women as equals. The man as the head of the house and the woman as the neck that turns the head.

"You have to learn how to submit," I told them. "The king needs his queen; there are certain things that he can't do. Anybody play chess?" I explained that in chess the queen is the most powerful piece on the board.

The hosts seemed to get what I was saying. We kept talking and laughing, and when the interview ended, I was happy with myself. We focused on my music, the conversation went well and was fun, we talked a lot about God, and I didn't get pulled into any catty drama—there was nothing for *MediaTakeOut* to run with.

But on the way to my car, I got a text from my hairdresser and bestie Derickus: "A lot of people are upset."

"About what?" I texted back.

Then he replied: "Submit??"

KENDALL

I was planning to accompany my wife to the interview, but instead I agreed to a meeting while we were already in New York for Fashion Week. I was at the hotel waiting for my wife to return, and I, too, began to see the negative backlash in the comments trending. By then I knew we had to do some damage control. And by that I mean I realized it was less about "control" than a need for "clarity." From Wendy Williams to Tavis Smiley, Erica Campbell's talk show and so many more, the statement my wife had made about submission was spreading like a wildfire. Our friends and family started to hit us up, and we also began to be sought out regarding additional interviews. I felt that it was important for me to communicate that my wife is a very powerful Black woman, and she was doing fine running her life before she ever met me; she didn't need me in her life to achieve great things because greatness had already been accomplished. But she is my wife, and as her husband, I felt a strong need to protect her in this uncomfortable moment.

FANTASIA

When Ken told me that my comments had gone viral, I started to get nervous; did I say something I didn't mean? The women who have followed my career know that I'm not someone who needs a man to tell her what to do.

KENDALL

The word "submit" comes with a lot of preconceived notions. A lot of women have been scarred, mentally, emotionally, and physically, because they relinquished control to a man who proved to be unworthy. But I'm no caveman, dragging my wife into a cave of my immaturity and selfishness, and I won't advocate for any man to act like that. It was clear that we needed to bring a little more clarity to the situation. Fantasia's submitting was now a national narrative, and the assumption was that it was a negative thing.

FANTASIA

For many women, and especially for Black women, "submit" tends to be a loaded word. Lots of us think it means to bow down, like, "Whatever he says goes; you cook the food and shut your mouth." They think submission equates to suppression, so some people thought I was stupid or repressed because of what I said. But that's not what happens in my house at all, and that's not what I said.

KENDALL

But when my wife shared her example on the radio, my particular portion of this conversation was missing. If a man goes on national radio and says he submits to his wife, no one's upset about it on Twitter. That's what a man in a good marriage does—and that's what I would have said if I had been there. But if a woman says the same thing, some people experience traumatic triggers.

So, I stepped way outside of my comfort zone and went online and posted a video. I basically said, "Let me tell you how it's supposed to work from a man's perspective." I explained how "submission" is a biblical word that God uses to instruct us about the balance in a healthy marriage. I said that submission requires trust; it is something that is earned. You can submit only to someone who is aligned with God.

When we met, Fantasia was carrying the world on her shoulders, handling her own just fine. She was hustling, paying her bills, being a good mother, and taking care of so many people. But she was able to off-load certain things to me that were weighing her down and preventing her from being the best person she could be. And I also could off-load certain things to her to create room for me to grow and expand into a better man as well. Individually and as a couple, we had done the work. Finally, the controversy began to pipe down and after the live video I presented, the feedback, comments, and support for our marriage exploded and increased unimaginably!

FANTASIA

Sometimes God has a sense of humor. I'd never heard Wendy Williams talk about God before, but she said that she agreed with me. Many other women began to comment, agreeing and showing support now that there was clarity around how submission functions in my marriage. Ken and I would be out to eat or shopping and we would have men and women in the grocery store coming up to me to give me a thumbs-up, and women would share their support. They would tell Ken, "Salute!"

KENDALL

Then something very interesting began to happen. Totally unrelated, just a few months earlier, we had started going live on Instagram with a little spiel to inspire people, especially couples who were married or in relationships. Just hopping in front of an iPhone and being real for sixty seconds. This week we would do a little spiel; the next week a little spiel. Then we started doing a little three-minute conversation. Then we started streaming live on Facebook at the same time. We called the segments *Taylor Talks*.

FANTASIA

They weren't deep philosophical discussions. We are not psychiatrists or licensed counselors. It's not like we've been therapists for twenty years. We are a real Black couple going through real-life things. But suddenly, after *Breakfast Club*, lots of people became curious about our marriage.

KENDALL

Because of my wife's work, we realize that people look at us as a power couple or a celebrity couple. They were curious about how submission plays out in our marriage and started sending us messages like, "Can we talk to y'all? We can see you're both very powerful; how do you make it work?"

FANTASIA

I'm a Cancer; I'm emotional; their messages touched me. I want to see every married person make their relationship work. My mother and father were together for twenty-seven years and then they got divorced. I wish they'd been able to work it out. Out of all my grandmother's grandkids, I'm the only one who's married. I've seen most marriages around me break. It seems like every day we hear a story about another couple going through a rocky moment or the kind of stuff that could lead to divorce. Many celebrity relationships are in trouble and that hurts me. I know lots of successful women, both inside and outside the entertainment industry, who want to have a good relationship but struggle to find one, or create one, or keep one. In general, lots of millennials aren't marrying.[1] And for lots of reasons—ranging from what it takes to overcome poverty, to trying to

---

1. Benjamin Gurrentz, "For Young Adults, Economic Security Matters for Marriage," June 26, 2018, United States Census Bureau, https://www.census.gov/library/stories /2018/06/millennial-marriages.html.

work and go to school, to needing to pay off college debt, to how hard it is to get a good job—this is especially true with Black millennials.[2] But in spite of all that, lots of people seemed to be very inspired by our marriage.

KENDALL

People want love. People want to be married. But they don't know how to do it—in part because they don't have people in their lives to give them real, true advice. Too many people think they can put their marriage in a microwave and get a positive result. But that's not how marriage works.

Our followers started asking us more and more questions, so we decided that we would go live and share our successes but also our mistakes: how we got through them, how we prayed through them, how we submitted to each other, and how we apologized and learned to forgive.

We wanted to be a celebrity couple willing to let others see humility and simplicity in the midst of having power, willing to let people see the human factor. Authenticity will always find its own audience.

FANTASIA

I've always been an open book. That's what soul singers are like. I sing what I feel, and that's how I live my life. I don't try to hide anything from the world and that frees me from my past. I'm never afraid to share personal things because, even though I won *Idol*, I don't want to be idolized. I'm human. I go through things just like everyone else does.

---

2. Amanda Barroso, Kim Parker, and Jesse Bennett, "As Millennials Near 40, They're Approaching Family Life Differently Than Previous Generations," May 27, 2020, Pew Research Center, https://www.pewresearch.org/social-trends/2020/05/27/as-millennials-near-40-theyre-approaching-family-life-differently-than-previous-generations/.

We wanted to be two authentic people in a world where so many people live behind filters and nobody wants to post a picture from a bad angle, much less talk about the broken places in their lives.

KENDALL

In *Taylor Talks*, we share our weaknesses, our scars, everything that stands in opposition to the way the entertainment industry operates. Not many public figures are willing to do that because they're afraid to show you any kind of chink in their armor. Most celebrities know their status can be fragile, so they are afraid they will tarnish their platform that can elevate them to a godlike stature—you have to be what people expect you to be so that people can live vicariously through you.

We let people see our humanity and flaws. We invite them into that sacred place of "I messed up, man. I was sleeping on the couch. Let me tell you what I did so that y'all don't make that mistake." I am open to putting my mistakes on the altar in hopes that doing so will benefit another man.

FANTASIA

People also knew we didn't start off with fancy-schmancy stories. I won *Idol* when I was only nineteen and have ministered to people and shared my gift, but I've also been burned, roasted, and dragged all through the media. Some of my most embarrassing, difficult, and even darkest moments have been presented to the public as entertainment.

Kendall has been convicted of three felonies, but that's not all of who he is. Before I met him, he had rebuilt his life and had a multi-million-dollar business. Today he has a ministry of leading men and working with people who have been incarcerated.

KENDALL

As I study our society and talk to men at all levels, all too often marriage is not appreciated. It's not protected, especially in our millennial generation. Many of us haven't seen a lot of success stories, expecially those who come from communities like Fantasia and I were raised in—places where many people struggle to make ends meet, the education isn't always the best, good job opportunities are scarce, and many men are swept into the criminal justice system.

So many couples conceal, they cheat, they have separate accounts, they have hidden accounts, their marriages are open, they swing, and they have hidden agendas.

FANTASIA

But here's the thing: I think most people out there know what's good, but many are too scared to do what's right. People are too nervous to let their guard down—like, all the way down.

KENDALL

With so many marriages at war, I believe our world is in danger. When marriages fail, you have more broken children, which leads to a broken economy, which leads to a broken society. In fact, you don't have to look far to see the distressing condition of so many of today's youth.

THE TAYLORS

There is purpose in marriage, so there's purpose in ours. In this season, we believe God is positioning us to be a model for others, even though we're still looking for models to follow. With so many people looking to us for inspiration, we feel called to make marriage our ministry. We want everyone to experience healthy relationships and to be living examples of how a righteous marriage is supposed to be designed and how it will survive. But we can't follow the same broken patterns that don't work throughout society, didn't work for our parents, or even the ones that didn't work for us in previous relationships. We think it's time to turn to some timeless principles that we believe position us to have a greater chance of success in love and in marriage.

It's a scary thing to put ourselves on the forefront of this important endeavor. We're still learning; we're still trying to figure it out. We're imperfect, and we're nervous that what we have to say might not be good enough. But we will not succumb to a spirit of fear that we might be criticized. We know we will be criticized. Real talk!

Our goal in this book is to move our readers beyond the mindset that marriage isn't possible, it isn't for you, it's too hard, or it's not worth the risk even to dream of getting married or to engage in the effort to make your marriage work. We prayed that as we participated in the process of writing the book that we, too, would be transformed. We expected that we would learn; we would grow; we would become stronger, closer, more whole, more aware—just as a result of engaging in the process. If we grew as we wrote it, we knew our book could be transformative to others. While writing it, we have become better as a man and a woman; closer as a husband and a wife; better parents; better leaders.

Though we are in counseling, we are not marriage counselors, therapists, or marriage experts. We do not think we have everything together. We are speaking real stuff to people like us who have been through real stuff. We're sharing what we've been through. We don't sugarcoat. We straight-up tell you when we think, *I probably could have done this differently. Let me give this another try.* We talk about our success but are not afraid to admit our mistakes. And we have had to do—and continue to do—a lot of apologizing and forgiving.

That said, we each have overcome tremendous obstacles and excelled in certain areas of life. For Fantasia, that has been as a vocalist and performer; for Ken, that has been in the world of business. In the process of growing, developing, and challenging ourselves to push outside of our respective comfort zones so we can reach higher levels professionally, we have experienced insights and learned skills that also serve us in marriage. Some of what we've learned in those areas might even help you. Just to give you an example, one of the most important things we've discovered is that it's important not to bring the "crowns" we have earned out in the world into our home. That's just one of many ways we protect ourselves from individualism, materialism, instant gratification, sexual temptation, and other destructive ideals that our society promotes but that could destroy our marriage. Even though we have both made mistakes, we have learned that our true crowns don't exist in earthly credentials but in each other and in developing the character we need to demonstrate to experience a righteous life and marriage. At the end of the day, the only credential that matters is the crown that God bestows upon you.

We believe God is using us as a weapon and a resource for righteous marriages. Our hope is that greater numbers of people will aspire to get married and will build and protect their marriage in a world where matrimony is not celebrated. In some of the *Taylor Talks*, we explore a topic people have been asking us about in an engaging, he said/she said style and reach a shared perspective—not of what Kendall thinks is best for him as an individual, or of what Fantasia thinks is best for her individually—but of what is best for us as a couple: Mr. and Mrs. Taylor. Because we have discovered that a strong relationship—and especially a strong marriage—allows us to free ourselves from some of the limitations that come with just being one person and opens up the new world of possibility and synergy that can take place when "me" and "me" transform into one "we."

We have organized the book according to the top ten topics that our followers tend to ask us about paired with our responses. Using our conversational *Taylor Talks* style, in each chapter we share a combination of our personal stories, spiritual principles, lessons we've learned, and insights we've reached along the way. We have learned some lessons the easy way, but many times God has chastised or even whupped us for some of our behavior and mistakes. We hope that by putting ourselves out there and being very vulnerable and transparent with the type of personal business that most people don't share, we will help you reflect on your own relationships—whether you're married, partnered, single, dating, or whatever—so that you experience stronger partnerships and marriages.

At the end of each chapter, we invite you to take some time to think about how some of the ideas we discuss might relate to or inspire you. Like many artists, Fantasia is very big on journaling, a practice of self-expression that can help you better understand your thoughts, feelings, and observations. She has creative journals, dream journals, and journals that she uses to capture her emotions. Journaling can be particularly helpful for creative types, who tend to use it to explore their thoughts and feelings, and catalog different ideas, images, sounds, and inspirations that might be meaningful later on. But one of the greatest works of art is the human relationship and family. We hope that putting pen to paper gives you greater clarity in imagining and creating a stronger relationship with God and a healthy partnership and family of your own.

Journaling can also help with our mental health. It can help put us in a better mood, give us a better sense of well-being, help us not feel as depressed before we have to handle the stressful parts of our lives, reduce some of the symptoms trauma often causes, and give us a place to download some of our mental clutter so we have a better memory.[3] At the end of each chapter, we also suggest some exercises that we hope will help you reflect upon and strengthen you and your relationship with your partner.

We strongly believe that the depth of your vulnerability with your partner will determine the highs you will be able to achieve in your marriage—and we want you to achieve the highest highs. So, we offer you our most vulnerable selves as our way of helping God build a kingdom of married people and others in strong romantic relationships who can learn and grow together and produce strong children and families.

---

3. Courtney E. Ackerman, "83 Benefits of Journaling for Depression, Anxiety, and Stress," July 15, 2021, PositivePsychology.com, https://positivepsychology.com/benefits-of -journaling/.

No
Crowns
in the
Castle

CHAPTER 1

"I DO"

Marriage at First Sight

FANTASIA

I was in Charlotte, at a spot called Fahrenheit, a classy place downtown on the rooftop of a hotel, hanging out with a few close friends. We were having a good time until a slightly drunk man came up and tried to holler at me. We started talking, and we soon realized that we both were originally from High Point, North Carolina. Now, even though I was enjoying talking to this guy named Jacob about High Point and reminiscing on the old days and various places where we both used to hang out, my friends were getting a little irritated and wanted to get back to our time together. My girl to the left kept nudging me on the leg, so I was thinking of how to wrap up the conversation without being rude.

KENDALL

"Orlando, who is your man Jacob over there talking to?" I asked. "Looks like he's trying to holler at a group of ladies at the bar."

"I have no clue. He's definitely had a few too many tonight, that's for sure," Orlando said.

"Well, besides that, how long are we planning to stay out tonight? You know I don't party like these young cats out here," I said.

"C'mon, bro, you just closed a major contract. We need to celebrate," Orlando replied.

"Facts, but you know after I've had a few drinks, I like to get back to hiding in the shadows. Matter fact, here comes Jacob now, and why is he smiling like he's up to something?" I asked.

"Yo! That's Fantasia, bruh! I bought them a few drinks and they said that they might head over to this spot called Suite. What y'all trying to do?" Jacob asked.

I laughed and said, "Man, we ain't about to be chasing no women around Charlotte. And that don't even look like Fantasia! Don't fool around and get catfished out here."

FANTASIA

"Friend, he doesn't even look like your type. Plus, he talks too much!" my friend said to me. "He's wasted, and if I was you and I had waited for seven months fasting, I would not waste my time on that."

True! I had just come off of a spiritual fast—no sex, no relationships, no drinking, listening to a lot of sermons and eating the word of God. I left a toxic relationship, put a ring on my own finger, and made a conscious effort to take time off from dating. I'll tell you more about that in a minute.

"Yeah, you're right, he's not my type. But maybe he would be a nice catch for you?" I said, and we both laughed. "They invited us to come over to Suite and said that the drinks are on them. Let's just go and check it out and whenever we say it's time, we can leave."

KENDALL

"How you even know that's the real Fantasia? I've seen pics of her back in the day and that ain't Fantasia!" I told Jacob. "And what makes you think you got a shot at that anyway?"

Everyone at my table laughed it off, but we were all in agreement about keeping the night going just a little bit longer. So, we paid for our food and drinks and then caravanned behind the ladies and headed over to Suite. It wasn't until we pulled up to the valet and everyone began yelling Fantasia's name and taking pics that I realized she really was who Jacob said she was. I immediately felt embarrassed by his drunken behavior and didn't want his actions to be seen as a reflection of me and the way I carried myself.

FANTASIA

We took the escalator up to Suite and by this time I was in a great mood and was feeling myself. I had just gotten back from being on the road doing my last Broadway play, *After Midnight*. The way Broadway works, you have two weeks to prepare. You have to learn all the steps, the music, your blocking, when the curtain comes down, how the set is moving. It's military-style. You have to be ready. Nothing can stand in the way. So after all that, I was ready to let my hair down—the little bit I have! I was in a mean pair of red bottoms, tight dress, and all my girls were looking good as well. Now, I was ready to go inside and turn up, but my girls were still shaky on me agreeing to Jacob's invite. So, we stood at the entrance debating if this was how we really wanted our night to end.

KENDALL

As I came up the escalator, I saw that the ladies were in a huddle standing by the entrance to the lounge. I'm very protective of my name and character, so I walked up to the group alone.

"Good evening, my name is Kendall. I want to apologize for how Jacob was acting at the other spot. I just want to state that it's not the character of the whole group. We don't want to impact you ladies' night, but if you do decide to come in, we will be sure that you have a nice time."

After they expressed their thanks, I walked back to my crew.

FANTASIA

I turned around to all my girls and said, "Hey, do y'all see what I just saw? I didn't see him at Fahrenheit; where was he hiding?" And before they could even reply I said, "Heaven, honey, heaven!"

They laughed at me and said, "Okay, girl, so what do you wanna do?"

"Let's go in, even if it's just for a little while," I said.

KENDALL

We were in Suite chilling and my man Orlando reserved a cabana and bottle service. Everyone was mingling and enjoying the night. The only thing on my mind at the time was the business deal that I had just closed and what my next moves would be. I had only one drink and was truly ready to go as soon as someone gave me the word.

I was glancing around the room and then I looked her way and locked eyes with Fantasia, who was sitting across the table and about four or five people away. We just stared at each other for a second. Then we both turned away. But then our eyes came right back to each other and this time she said, "SMILE." In that moment I realized I must have had a serious look on my face. Sitting there looking at her amazing smile, all I could do was smile back.

FANTASIA

The entire time that I'm sitting there, it was like I had zoned out from everything else going on around me. The club was loud, bodies were moving everywhere, and the energy was all over the place. But my attention was on how Kendall was sitting there, clearly not wanting to be there. He wasn't acting like the other guys in his group or most men that I've been around.

I reached over and whispered to one of my male friends, "I really want to talk to that guy over there. But it's been so long since I've talked to any man and I'm not about to go up to approach him. I don't know?"

As soon as I said this, my favorite song at the time came on, "We Dem Boyz" by Wiz Khalifa. So, I grabbed my girls, and we all went straight to the dance floor.

Turn up, turn up, turn up!

KENDALL

The ladies bolted to the dance floor when Wiz Khalifa came on. That joint did hit pretty hard during that time. There was one guy in their group who kept trying to get my attention. When I finally acknowledged him, he nodded his head toward the dance floor like, "Go over there." At first, I didn't catch on to what he was hinting at.

Then he whispered across the table, "Fantasia wants to talk to you."

"Me?" I asked.

"Yeah, you."

"You serious? I don't play games," I said, not wanting to be embarrassed.

"I'm serious; she wants you to talk to her," he replied.

I sat there for a second trying to wrap my head around this entire night. I debated whether she was genuinely interested in me or just wanted company for that night alone. I wasn't about to be a boy toy or just some fun for the evening. But I shook it off and was like, "Whatever, let's do it!"

The dance floor was jam-packed, with bodies everywhere and hands in the air. I couldn't even find her at first. Then when a few people put their hands down—yeah, it was that crazy in there—I saw her in the middle of the crowd dancing and having a great time. I had already introduced myself outside, and I'm not a dancer. So, I pushed my way through the crowd until I was standing right behind her. She couldn't see me. I wrapped my hands around her waist, and I snatched her toward me. She turned around and was startled, of course.

"Boy!" she yelled until she realized it was me. Then she produced the biggest smile.

"I just wanted to see what was up," I said. "I'll be out there when you get done dancing."

FANTASIA

We talked all the way until the sun came up. We talked about everything—about family, our relentless spirits in business, the many things that had tried to destroy us, and our desire for something new and different from what we had both experienced in our pasts.

We both were hesitant and, to be honest, I think we both were a little scared to entertain the idea of something serious at that time. It was clear that we both were in a space of self-protection and both had a sense of self-worth. But the energy, the sparks, and this feeling of comfort kept pushing me to move beyond those fears, and to be open-minded, and to keep my heart open to the spirit of "what could be." This was different. It just felt so different to me.

KENDALL

A few days later, she invited me to the Great Wolf Lodge, an indoor family water park in Concord, North Carolina. She said she was taking her kids and a friend of hers and invited me to join her. We hadn't spoken for a few days since the night at Suite, and I was still curious about her and wanted to learn more. I walked inside the water park and began looking for her. At first, I couldn't find her. Déjà vu, right? There were kids everywhere and water splashing on me from every crack and crevice. I literally felt like the fish who was out of water. While looking for Fantasia, I saw this woman get out of the pool, and let's just say my search was temporarily disrupted by this amazing distraction! Hey, I mean I was single at the time, right?

"Ain't that a shame! You supposed to be looking for me and you were out there looking at other women," Fantasia said. "Funny when you found out it was me hopping out that pool, huh?!"

Now I was definitely glad I made the trip!

FANTASIA

Now, the whole time he had been looking for me, I was looking at him and I remember to this day what he had on: a white tee, black gym shorts, black Jordans, and a black hat.

He then told me that he had to take a call about a family reunion. I thought that was pretty cool, because I could tell he didn't want me to get the wrong idea about him being on the phone. He even sat next to the pool and took his call, I guess to prove to me that it was what he said it was. I was also taking notes because I personally don't know many men who sit in on family reunion calls. So, the fact that family was important to him was another positive box checked off for me. I was also cool with it because it gave me more time to check him out. I don't know why, but for the life of me I remembered him being short that night at Suite. Maybe it was the six-inch heels I had on or the ego I was wearing that night, but I really thought he was short. But, oh my, how wrong I was!

I pulled my girlfriend to the side. "Girl, he don't even know it yet, but that's my boyfriend right there!" And we both just laughed.

I got out of the pool and we got all the kids together and headed upstairs to eat. Kendall came up with me and I introduced him to everyone there. I told him that I needed to take a shower really quick. He said that he would wait in the lounge area and check some emails until I was ready.

KENDALL

While I was sitting in the lounge area checking emails, I started looking around. It was my first time at the Great Wolf Lodge. I'm sitting here, looking through my businessman's lens at the infrastructure and layout of this place in amazement. The way they embraced technology and made it kid-friendly, charging an arm and a leg for the rooms, all of the souvenirs and gadgets, et cetera. This is just how my mind works. I sit or visit a place and my mind immediately begins to break down and analyze "how."

FANTASIA

Wait a minute. So, you're telling me that the whole time I'm rushing myself to shower and get out there to you, hoping you're not out there feeling like I left you stranded and alone, you were trying to figure out business stuff instead of thinking about me?

KENDALL

Of course I was thinking about you. I had you on the brain, Queen, but my brain is just wired the way it is. Can I finish?

FANTASIA

I guess…

KENDALL

So, as I was saying, I'm sitting there waiting on her to finish show-ering and then she comes around the corner in this long blue dress with a matching hat. She's never been more beautiful to me than in that very moment. No makeup, no fans, and no entourage. Just her brilliant smile, her dark skin, and her peaceful presence. She apolo-gized for taking so long and we began to talk.

FANTASIA

I took what I know was the quickest shower ever in my life! I was a little nervous, and I was asking my friend and daughter if I looked okay, and if my dress needed to be ironed—you know, girly stuff. Kinda reminds me of a few of the lyrics from "When I See U"! I couldn't shake the nervous feeling. Usually, I am a ball of confidence when it comes to these kinds of things, and I didn't understand why I couldn't control this feeling in my stomach. I figured that since I'm usually the one being interviewed and hit with tons of questions because I'm an entertainer, this time I would sit back and let Kendall do most of the talking. And so that's exactly what I did.

I asked him, "Tell me something about you that you normally wouldn't tell people you've just met."

KENDALL

"That's a pretty loaded question," I said. "Well, I was born in Germany. My mother and father were in the military and that's where I jumped on the scene. Never knew my father. He left my mother before I was one year old, but I'm sure you've heard that kind of story before. A few years after that, my mom was diagnosed with Hodgkin's cancer. I went to live with my grandmother in Chicago while my mother was in the hospital. It was a little over a year before she would come home, but not without having to put on the fight of her life to beat it."

"Wow, I'm sorry to hear that," Fantasia responded sympathetically.

"Yeah, it's crazy to reflect on the stories she has shared about how painful and gruesome the operations and chemotherapy were," I said. "She told me of a time that I visited her in the hospital, and I kept asking her when she would be coming home. She said that was the extra push that she needed to endure those procedures when she felt at times it would be better to just let go."

"We take so much in life for granted," Fantasia responded. "We really do. Are y'all still close?"

"Oh yeah. That's my homie right there," I said, sitting back in my chair, feeling more comfortable. "I feel insanely comfortable talking to you. It's weird. You have honest eyes."

"No, you got the nice eyes. They are pretty."

"Pretty? Nothing about me is pretty."

"You know what I mean, boy, keep talking," Fantasia said sassily.

"Well, I never had a true father figure. Ever. From an early age I had to become the man of the house. My mother eventually married again, but that didn't work out as they planned. Many things impacted our home during those years. I saw, heard, and learned a lot very early in my life. In school, well, school was never a challenge class-wise. I would complete my homework before class ended or, worst case, on the bus after school. Looking back, I wasn't really being challenged and I think that played a role in me looking outside in the world for that sense of challenge. And like so many young Black boys seeking a challenge, I found it in the streets."

"So, you were that smart but still were drawn to the streets?" she asked. "And what do you mean exactly? You don't look anything like a street dude to me."

"Oh, trust me," I continued. "I don't look like the scars that I carry. I had my son Treyshaun—yes, I have a son. I had him when I was only fifteen. Around this time is when I began selling drugs. I was expelled from every school in the city of Gastonia, North Carolina, by age sixteen. Within the same year I was in a shoot-out that left me shot twice. I still carry a bullet in my left lung. At age seventeen, I was forced to leave my mother's home after the feds came and searched my house for weapons and drugs. Shortly after I was convicted of another felony charge. And…"

"Wait a minute, hold up! You were shot? Sold drugs, felonies? I can't picture you doing any of those things."

"I know, right!" I replied. "I think that used to help me during all those court dates. I would throw on a shirt and tie and even the judges couldn't wrap their mind around the charges being mentioned and the fact that I was attached to them. Yes, God has been covering me through a lot of my mistakes. But I eventually took my mom's advice and moved to Charlotte to try to find a new path for myself. She used to beg me to get my GED, which I didn't see any value in. I finally agreed, and I got my GED in two days, and gave it to her. I haven't seen it since."

"How can you get a GED in two days?" Fantasia asked suspiciously.

"Well, I was trying to stop selling drugs, so I was working two jobs at the same time when I was nineteen. I was waiting tables in the daytime at Souper Salad, and then I was an alley coordinator for Red Lobster at night. I went to Central Piedmont Community College and I took the placement tests they give you to determine where you need help and which class to place you in. I scored high enough on my placement test where they agreed to let me just test completely out. The challenge was that I had one day where I was off on both jobs, and though they didn't recommend it, they agreed to let me sit all day and take all of the individual tests at one time. That was a long day! But I scored high enough on all the first tests that, by the time they got to the reading and literature, they told me I had already passed. So, yeah, two days!"

"You are blowing my mind. I am trying to process all of this. All I can say is, wow!"

"I know, it's a lot for a first date, huh?" I said with a smile.

"Oh, so we on a date now?" Fantasia asked.

"I guess we'll see. But I've given you a lot about me and my past, but I don't know much about you and yours. Tell me something about you that you normally wouldn't share on a first date."

"Really? All of my business and life is all on the internet already."

"But I haven't read anything about you," I said. "If I can be honest, the night that we first met, I didn't think you actually were who you are."

"What do you mean?" she asked.

"I mean, in person you don't look anything like the pictures that I've seen. At all."

"I don't take that as a compliment, but okay."

"Just saying, your pictures just don't capture your beauty. That's all I'm saying."

"Oh, you smooth with it!" she said. "Umm, well I can share this: I was in a lot of money issues for a while and I'm proud of myself. I had to work out of a one-million-dollar hole in taxes, and I just paid it all off. That, for me, is something that I am proud of accomplishing and something I normally wouldn't share with someone new. I really like talking with you. I really do. Maybe we can do this again sometime soon."

"I enjoyed this too," I answered. "And I'm cool with connecting again. I just want to be honest and say that I'm focused on running my company and not really in a place for a serious relationship. I believe in being honest and not playing with people when there is no need to."

"So, you are saying that you ain't trying to date, that's what you're telling me?"

"Basically," I told her. "I am cool with friends and getting to know people, but I don't want to be misleading and be looked at as one of those kinda guys."

"Yeah, okay, I hear you. We will be seeing each other again."

KENDALL

Our moments of transparency were so important. At first, I'd just figured she liked "bad guys." But each of us had sacrificed to build multimillion-dollar brands and companies, and that's how we identified ourselves at that point. When we sat there and we put all of our bs out there, it's like we were playing show-and-tell without knowing it.

FANTASIA

It was intentional for me because I felt like I kept getting into relationships pretending to be what they wanted, and not being who I was. Kendall and I started it off with "I am telling this and I am telling that because I would rather for you to hear it from me." I wasn't afraid. I told him stuff about the issues I'd had earlier in my life education-wise, how growing up music was bigger in our family's home than education; how I wouldn't get my homework done because I was up late singing. Those seven months of fasting allowed me to see that I was beautifully made and fine just the way I was, flaws and all. And if someone's going to love you, they're going to love the entire package. Plus, nobody could come back and be like, "Oh, guess what I heard." It made me feel so much better because I felt like, "You ain't got no secrets on me. You cannot go take that and turn it into a joke." Let us just be honest.

KENDALL

Nobody really said, "Hey, let's do this transparency thing," but we just started saying, "Look, this is what I been through"; "Well, this is what I been through"; "Well, I'm gonna go ahead and tell you this"; "Well, I'm gonna tell you that." We had so many things in common on both the positive and the negative aspects of our lives.

FANTASIA

Ladies, PLEASE hear me!! Understand that after sitting with this man—a Real Man, who spoke so well, smelled so good, who looked me in my eyes the entire time while never making a sexual pass at me—I thought about him even more. Now, I was curious—curious to see how he would carry himself in my world and atmosphere and how he would deal with all the commotion that surrounds me on a daily basis. So I invited him to my birthday party in DC for our next date. Why DC? Because I love go-go music. I could already tell he really cared nothing about all the lights, and the hype, and all the noise. I mean, come on now, you heard the list of red flags he gave me on our first date. This man's wall was up high, and it was a Great Big Wall.

Now, I already told you that before coming home to North Carolina and meeting my future husband (wink, wink), I had been on a very strong dating fast. I was living in New York City for about seven months, doing *After Midnight* on Broadway. It was a great time for me to totally focus on myself and allow myself to heal and figure some things out. I won't even bring up my past relationships here, because to me, especially in the place I'm in right now, they don't deserve the acknowledgment. But I needed some time with myself and away from men, so I decided to take a break.

I finally decided to do me, which is crazy because I wrote a song about that long ago ("I'm Doin' Me"). Guess I was still in that place lots of women are in now, which is just wanting love so bad, and wanting it right then and there. *After Midnight* was a different kind of role for me. It wasn't like playing Celie from *The Color Purple*, or even like when I played myself in my own Lifetime movie. This character was free and fun and very confident, so I was able to put myself in that type of headspace.

Committing to being single was a chance for me to learn to love Fantasia again. I did a lot of emotional releasing and letting go. I began to heal, grow, and educate myself in so many areas, while also preparing for the true love that my Father in heaven had waiting for me. During my fast, I took the time to assess what I was really looking for in a partner. I'd tell God, "You know what I need, but I think You're testing me to see if I know what I need." I needed a man to heal my heart and be a father to my kids. A praying man. A man who was intelligent, patient, and kind. I wanted a man who was wise, God-fearing, and had a calm demeanor. Someone who could see me, not just a girl on a stage. Someone special, not like the guys I'd dated before. I began writing these things down on sticky notes and index cards and taping them all over my dressing room.

I had men hitting on me back-to-back, but I stuck to my personal vows. The fasting allowed me to say to myself, *You are beautifully made; you are fine just the way you are, flaws and all. If somebody's gonna love you they're gonna love the whole entire package.* And as I fell in love with myself, I fell back in love with the industry that I'd been angry with for taking advantage of me—a gullible Southern teenager with an amazing gift. After a while I even felt like, "I'm gonna be that artist that's cool with being alone right now." I almost felt like I might be okay by myself. I'm gonna be singing "Free Yourself" and "Bittersweet" for the rest of my life, real talk. So I was like, "This is it for me, and if I gotta sing it, doggone it, I'll sing it good."

I started to understand that God could not release certain blessings or open certain doors regarding love because I wasn't ready. Had I gotten the right man at the wrong time, I probably would have pushed him away. For real. The Father can't bless mess and, boy, was my life pretty messy.

So after choosing myself and going through that process, I felt like I had already seen so much in Kendall—or Ken Doll, which is what I started calling him the day I met him. Why? Well, meeting him reminded me of the times I would play with my dolls as a little girl, and I would always make sure my Ken doll was protecting and treating the family well. My Ken doll loved Barbie and would do anything for her. It was already a fantasy I had carved in my mind as a little girl. The crazy part was, I never really focused on the marriage part in my fantasy world, just protection. Hmm!! That says a lot, right?! Long story short, I wanted to spend more time with him, and see if this feeling I was feeling was different, or if it was that same feeling of forcing love that I had created a pattern of in my past.

KENDALL

I have to be honest. When she asked me to consider coming to her birthday party, I was closed-minded. Not because I didn't want to see her again, but because I don't like to drive. At all. I prefer to fly when possible, and the thought of a six-hour drive each way to see someone that lives in my own city wasn't something I immediately jumped at. Plus, remember that we had just met, and I didn't understand how I would fit into her birthday bash, not knowing any of her close friends and family at the time. But, just like the night I pulled her close at Suite, I said, "Whatever, let's do it."

My close friend and brother, Yael, was the main one telling me that I should go and that she could be "the one." I was confused because he knew better than most about my position on being in a serious relationship at that time. Yet, he was so persistent and adamant about me going—to the point of agreeing to come with me just to sweeten the deal. We hit the road to DC, and I met up with her at her hotel. The way she smiled and greeted me when I walked in just kept humbling my pride and making me feel like I needed to be close to her. We chatted briefly, and then I excused myself, so that she and her glam team—which, that part was very new to me—could get things in order for the evening. Yael and I checked into our room, got dressed for the party, and headed to the bar, where I had my customary old-fashioned and just relaxed awhile. To my surprise, I saw Jacob walking into the hotel with Fantasia's friend from that night at Suite. I was bugging! I made sure I spoke, and then we both went back to our own rhythm. Interesting, huh?

I think it is important for me to take a moment to define what a birthday party meant to me prior to this night. Usually, some folks showed up, there was cake and ice cream, music, drinks, and laughter. But nah…not tonight! We pulled up to a full theater. The valet was stressing, and guests were lined up all around the building. I recall giving Yael this look, letting him know I felt that I had been set up. But the night went on and 112 hit the stage, Tweet hit the stage, and then other artists. I was taking this all in, silently, asking myself, *Is this her everyday life? Is this the norm, and if so, where would I fit in?* These were the things roaming through my head, all while 112 was singing "Peaches & Cream."

Now it was time for Fantasia and her band to hit the stage and, of course, I had never witnessed her singing live. I did not know all that was incorporated into her live show. I also had not seen any of her *Idol* performances, so I was truly in the dark as to what was about to happen. She hit the stage and I saw something my mind couldn't equate with the gentle and sweet little voice that I talked with at the Great Wolf. Here was this electric Black woman who was belting out these notes and commanding attention from everyone present. She had the hearts of everyone present in the palms of her hands. She was powerful, confident, sexy, fearless, unapologetic, and breathtaking!

And while I was already trying to process the atmosphere I'd found myself in, she went into "When I See U" and I literally had to sit down. Luckily, I was sitting in the highest section in the theater, where I could still clearly see the stage, because anywhere below where I was sitting, everyone was on their feet.

Absolutely insane!

Then there was a moment when she was talking to the crowd and those she labeled as "too-good-to-stand-up-and-have-a-good-time" kinda folks. So, I stood up, not wanting to appear as if I was the leader of the bunch. And all the way up from the nosebleed seats, we made eye contact, just as we did at Suite. She stopped singing and placed the mic by her side. I stood up in my seat, looking down, and I saluted her. She sent me a thousand-watt smile in return. She then lifted her hand and saluted me right back. Even with everything that was taking place around us, our spiritual connection had created an island of its own. And that is when I felt an undeniable sense of responsibility to spiritually cover and protect her. I now knew exactly where I would fit in.

FANTASIA

When he stood up on his seat, it hit a little different for me. See, in that very moment the Spirit had fallen on me. For some of you who don't know my backstory, let me fill you in on what I mean by this. God uses me in such a unique way onstage, and when His

Spirit hits me, I completely zone out. I feel His peace, power, and healing flow through the hearts of so many broken people who are in the audience, though I may not be actually looking at them while I'm singing. I felt such a deep focus and connection with Kendall in that moment, where everything and everyone else was blocked out. It was a feeling of God's presence and love that is still hard for me to describe. After the show, a large group of us drove to my manager's home, and Kendall and I found a quiet room and retreated there with our food and drinks. I shared my experience with him.

"Why did you feel the need to stand up at the time, and what did you see?" I asked him.

"I don't normally go out of my way to be seen and had no clue that you would even notice me," Kendall replied. "I was in a crowd of thousands, and you didn't know what tickets I was given, or where my seat was located. Yet, and still, I stood on top of the chair—maybe that helped a little—and when I knew that you noticed me, I wanted you to know that I saw you. And I don't mean that I recognized you. I mean that I saw who you were inside, and who you are to God. I understood that being different and carrying a divine gift can be lonely at times. Well, that's until you come in contact with someone who carries a spiritual gift just as you do."

KENDALL

Later that night, when I was on my way out the door, Derickus handed me a little bag. When I got home, I opened it up; it contained women's jewelry. I was confused but held on to it, thinking he had wanted to keep it safe but had made a mistake and given it to the wrong person. But the more I thought about it, I realized he could have kept the items himself but had handed them to me. Interesting.

FANTASIA

The party was so much fun, nicely put together, and it didn't stop there. My friends had an amazing trip to Cancun planned for me the next day, for an entire week. To be honest, I would have been at peace missing my flight just to be with Kendall one more day. And that is saying a lot, because I am deeply drawn to island vibes and water. But he was like a breath of fresh air that blew away everything toxic surrounding me, because around him everything just felt so clear. And for this reason, I wanted more time with him. I enjoyed myself out of the country, but I stayed on FaceTime with him nearly the entire time! My friends were not happy when I would want to go in early, or declined to go on certain excursions, but I couldn't help it. His spirit was like a magnet, and I was drawn into his conversations and energy. I asked him if he would like to spend more time with me when I got back into Charlotte.

KENDALL

Which I did want to do. In fact, she had tried to convince me to pack up and meet her in Cancun. I was just trying to register how any of this made sense. I felt like I was crashing party after party, being the new guy on the block, and I definitely wasn't trying to be a third leg on a birthday trip.

My saving grace was that I had never had a passport. I was still finishing my last years of probation from my last charge, and obtaining a passport was out of the question. I had spent years under the radar of the system, and the only loophole I'd found was that I could take a cruise that left out from the States, and I had been able to visit the Bahamas and Puerto Rico. But to catch a direct flight to connect with her in Cancun was not possible.

Back home, I would think about her a lot and try to make sense of this unusual feeling of wanting her close to me. I began to go online in hopes of learning more about her, but she cautioned me against it when I mentioned it to her. Yes, there were things and write-ups out there that didn't aim to paint her in a respectful light. But no article could turn me away from her when I had my criminal rap sheet out there as well. This only made the connection grow stronger and my curiosity to be heightened even more. She told me that she would be flying back and landing the next day, and I offered to shut down work early and come scoop her up from the airport.

FANTASIA

I was feeling like a little girl. He was COMING TO PICK ME UP!

"Derickus, I need you to do my hair! Somebody, help me put on a light beat. Please help me decide, what should I wear?" Now, I was doing all of this, having a full-on panic attack, and Derickus, who is my good friend, pulled me to the side and reminded me of something.

"Baby, show him who you really are," he said. "Remember all the things you gained from the fast and the alone time. You are looking for someone to see you and not all this stuff."

He was right! This guy was different, and I needed to just be 'Tasia without all the glitz and glam.

KENDALL

I pulled up to the airport, having made sure that I would arrive well before her flight landed. The only thing that was playing in my mind was whether or not I should have driven my Impala. I had a Chevy on 22s, and I wasn't sure if this was the manner in which I should pick up a woman of her caliber in public, and I began to regret that I didn't just drive my Tahoe instead. But as soon as she and her crew came out through the arrivals gate, that smile of hers blew all concern and worry right out of the tinted windows.

I pulled up to the curb and got out to open the door for her. Before she got in, I handed her the small bag that contained all the jewelry that she had mistakenly left behind in DC. By this point, I had realized it had been a tactful ploy that almost guaranteed I would have to see her in person again.

She waved her crew good-bye, hopped in the car, and I closed the door behind her. She was officially now in my world and space. Before I placed the car in drive, I looked her in the eyes, and I said, "Welcome home, beautiful. Are you hungry?"

FANTASIA

Of course, I said yes! I am a Southern girl, and I Can Eat! I felt like I was back in High Point again, feeling like the young, fun, and free Fantasia I used to be, and the one I missed. I mean, don't get me wrong, I'm still that girl, but there are certain areas of my life and personality that I keep hidden because all eyes are always on me.

Ken pulling up in his Impala and getting out with so much confidence was everything for me. His car reminded me of the first car I bought myself after winning *Idol*. It was a Chrysler 300 with some nice BIG wheels! You can't picture me riding tall on those big rims, huh? It's true. Look, I've had men send for me in limousines, and I hated it! I had no other choice but to wonder what their motives truly were, because that told me they were showing off. I am just a simple girl who does like nice things from time to time, but none of that makes or defines me. It doesn't bring me joy, nor does it "tickle my fancy," as Grandma would say.

My grandmother used to say that I should be cautious when

people flash what they have before showing me who they are. I believe that when men are flashy, it can come from only one of two places: either your hands are touching things that are harmful to the soul, or you have not fought through temptation and allowed God to keep you humble in your heart where you no longer seek validation hidden inside of material things.

When a man starts showing off before his character has a chance to shine first, it lets a woman know a lot about him, but the crazy thing is many women will still fall for this type of approach. I have dated several high-profile guys before. I've learned that guys who flash money, cars, jewelry, and stuff like that aren't really looking for a serious relationship. Nine times out of ten, when you fly out after a visit there is another woman flying in. Guys who are serious and really trying to build something are usually trying to protect what they have and are more cautious about who they invite into their financial world. At this point in my life, I was looking for the complete body of work, the crown visible outside that reflected the king that only I could see deep down on the inside. I could tell from the moment Kendall picked me up that I was in the presence of a real North Carolinian Man with a capital *M*.

KENDALL

We called a soul food spot close by for a take-out order. We walked into my place and she couldn't stop talking about how clean my spot was. She even made mention that I must have just moved in, but I informed her that I'd been there for a few years. My mother raised me to know how to cook, clean, do my own laundry, iron my clothes, and so on. She taught me that I never wanted to be a man who was dependent on a woman to be cared for, and that if I was able to care for myself, I could be more selective in the woman that I chose to be with. That always stuck with me and I valued that lesson, since she not only said it, but she would also teach me how to do the very things she wanted me to be able to do for myself.

"I see you have a Bible on your desk over there," Fantasia said. "I can tell by how it's looking that you really read your Bible."

"Of course," I replied. "This is the blueprint that I follow as a man. The more I learn, the more I realize how much I still don't know. Guess that's why the Scriptures state that with much wisdom comes grief and heavy burdens."

"Yeah, your Bible is all marked up and worn out. Not like those people who have Bibles just as ornaments like they do at hotels and stuff."

"Nah. Not me, lil lady. I have definitely learned to fear the Lord!"

"You play chess too?" she asked, pointing to a set on a table in the middle of the living room.

"Indeed. My mother began to teach me when I was around five or maybe six years old. She taught me early, and I've always approached life and decisions like chess moves. You know, thinking and looking three moves ahead at all times."

"I have always been curious about chess. Maybe one day you can teach me how to play?"

"Why wait?" I asked, walking over to the table. "Today is always a good time to learn something new. Check it: Each side has the same agenda, and that is to corner the opposing king the quickest. Each side has the same number and type of pieces, so the scales are balanced on both ends. No one side has an advantage at the beginning. The advantage has to be formed creatively by breaking down your opponent's agenda, and basically undermining it with your strategy. That make sense?"

"I think so," she replied. "Basically, you have to use these pieces to break down their pieces and take over?"

"That's it. It's a game of mental warfare. And that's how I look at life. You can set up the board for hours and make one wrong decision, one simple mistake, and it will cost you the entire game."

"Oh, that's dope!" she said excitedly. "No one has ever sat me down and taught me anything like this. I think I can beat you one day!"

She started dancing and pointing her fingers in my face, taunting.

"Slow down, lil mama," I said. "Pump those brakes, speed racer. Nothing but smoke over here waiting for you."

We shared a good laugh and romantic glances back and forth.

"Anyways, I have to fly out for a show tomorrow, but I'll be right back." She made a sad face and looked at me with puppy eyes. "I'm really going to miss you. Yes, I said it."

"I'm going to miss you, too, kiddo. But before you leave, I need to do something really quick. I'll be right back."

I went into my bedroom and returned with a small glass container of oil. Then I knelt down in front of her and opened the lid to the glass jar. I placed a small portion of the oil in my palm and rubbed it between both hands. I placed my fingertip on her forehead, her ears, her eyelids, her nose, the corners of her mouth, her heart, her hands. I then placed both of my hands on her feet and began to pray.

"Father, You are God and God alone. You are the Creator of all that is great and powerful. You are the giver of every good and perfect gift. There is none greater and none worthier than You. You are the Great I AM. I first ask You to forgive me of any and all sins that I have committed knowingly or unknowingly. I ask that You remove anything in or on me that would hinder these words from reaching Your throne of grace and mercy. And if it's Your will, please heed these words that are flowing from the depths of my heart. I pray over Fantasia as she travels as a light into dark places. She is an angel on this earth and a messenger of Your love and peace. I stand in the gap and cover her where she is exposed. I ask with all of the power You have imparted into me that You will shield her from all hurt, danger, confusion, and anything that stands against Your perfect will and promise. After she has completed what You are sending her for, I ask You, Lord, that You would be gracious enough to return her back to me. In Your Son Yeshuah's name, I ask, believe, and expect. Amen.

FANTASIA

Is this really happening? I thought.

While he was praying, so was I, because I was absolutely blown away. This was it. This right here was what I'd asked the Master for. This was what I was fasting for, this was what I wrote on all those sticky notes!

"Listen to what he is saying, Father! Wait, is Your hand in this? Wait, is this a trick? Am I being punk'd? I finally stepped out of Your way and I allowed You to lead and guide all of my next moves. Or should I say, Your next moves for me, Father. So, it's not a trick, but it's Your will for my life and this time I won't remove my spiritual ears or eyes to try to do it the way I want. Your will is what I pray will continue to be done in my life. AMEN!"

By the time I was done praying he was done as well, but his eyes were still closed, and I could tell he really meant every word he'd said. Before I knew it, a tear fell from my eye, down my face, and onto the top of his bald head. He looked up at me and asked, "Why are you crying?" He stood up and took his finger to dry my eyes, and my heart skipped several beats. It felt like we both had been here in this moment before. As if we had already been right here in this very same space. My Black Barbie moment had finally come to real life. As I ran through the mental list of all the traits I was looking for in a partner, all the things I had written about were the things Ken did. Number one was a man who loves the Word of God and loves God. He met all the requirements. I saw the king in him. And he was everything I'd been looking for—a man to see 'Tasia Monique, not FANTASIA! the woman who performs on a stage. You know what I mean?

I could tell this next show I had coming up was going to be a special one, and now I was going to cut all the way up! I clapped my hands and yelled, "Yeah!" exactly the way I do onstage.

KENDALL

The entire time that she was gone, we stayed connected. She called me after she got checked in through TSA, and again once she boarded the plane. I prayed for her peace and assurance during her flight. She contacted me to confirm she had landed and once again when she checked into her hotel. She had an amazing show, and the feedback in the media and social platforms was nothing but positive. When she returned, I met her at her home, and we found ourselves again nestled into a quiet place of talking and what I consider verbal intimacy.

FANTASIA

I continued telling him about some of the difficult things in my past. I wasn't afraid. I wanted him to know the real me so just in case he said, "I can't rock with you," then fine, let's not waste any more of each other's time. But he kept opening up about his struggles too.

KENDALL

I'd been on a fast of my own, though it slightly varied from that of my future wife's. When I got out of jail, I did nothing but work eighty-eight-hour weeks, focused on my pursuit of wisdom and spiritual and professional development; and tried to build a stronger relationship with my son.

FANTASIA

We had so much in common. I could see that he was a hustler; I'm a hustler. We'd both been at rock bottom and humiliated; we'd both come back from it like phoenixes out of the ashes. I fell in love with his story. I had never met anyone whose story was like mine before. I understood what he was going through and I knew he understood what I was going through. I was like, "Wow, so you never gave up…" 'Cause my grandmother would always tell me, when you fall down, get back up. I just kept hearing how he would fall down, and then get back up. Wow, somebody like me.

KENDALL

We're both two kids who came from nothing, who got everything that they have on their own, nothing handed out. We've both been broken down, built up, then broken down and built up again. Those are the things that we loved about each other. Ironic how our paralleling brokenness became the very building blocks of our much-needed sense of trust and loyalty. Life had tried to break both of us. Life had tried to drain us, make us think we were not who we are, and put us in a place where others could just extract from us time and time again. That day, we also started talking about some of our long-term goals. I think we knew it wasn't a game, it wasn't a gimmick, it wasn't that puppy love feeling; it was bigger than that. We trusted what our spirits were telling us.

FANTASIA

At one point I told him, "I love you; I can tell that I truly love you!"

KENDALL

Her voice sounded certain but there was subtle fear flickering in her eyes.

"I love you too," I told her. Then I took her hand and pulled her closer. "How would you describe the love you have for me? How does it differ from any other time you believed that you loved a man in your past?"

FANTASIA

"I love you in a way I could never have loved them," I told him. "I love you enough to become your wife."

Kendall didn't immediately respond. He sat silently for a moment, and this caused anxiety to creep into my heart.

KENDALL

I knew in this moment that my world was coming to a slow stop, and if I made this decision, my world would begin spinning in the opposite direction. And I had no clue or guarantees of what this new direction would look like, or the speed with which our new world would spin. The logical part of me was sending off alarms that this was the point of no return, where I could press pause and begin to exercise control over the matter, which was my comfort zone. At the same time, I knew that I had the ability to protect and lead her. I believed in my spirit that if I did not step up and become the covering she needed and deserved, and if anything negative happened to her after that moment, it would fall on me and that blood would be on my hands.

I also didn't want another man to have her, ever again. This—whatever this feeling was that her spirit was bringing into my life—I wanted to own it and to have it to myself alone. So, I asked her, "What do you have planned for the rest of your life?"

"Okay, so now I'm nervous," she replied. "What are you thinking?"

"Let's get married. I want you to carry my last name."

"Stop playing with me!" She pulled her hands back and went into protection mode.

I reached back for her hand and said, "Marry me, Fantasia."

"Are you sure? You promise?"

"Yes. I am not like these other men out here. I am a true man of God and a man of my word. So, what's up? Will you marry me?"

"Yes! Yes! Yes!" She jumped into my arms and began to cry uncontrollably. I held her tight for what felt like an eternity.

FANTASIA

It was important to us to settle into marriage in privacy, without the public becoming aware sooner than necessary because after all, we had only known each other for a total of three weeks. We knew that keeping our wedding a secret would require us to exchange vows outside of North Carolina where we both lived. So we decided to sneak away and get married in a courthouse located in Bennettsville, South Carolina, where my mother was born and grew up. The only people who knew were both of our moms, our kids, and my manager at the time.

At first when we walked into the courthouse, no one recognized me. It wasn't until we were officially married and walking out holding hands that the whispers started about a possible celebrity who had just tied the knot. Ken and I rushed to the Range Rover parked outside and drove off before anyone could take any pictures and release them on social media.

"Yo, that was close!" Kendall laughed, looking back at spectators trying to get a closer look as our SUV turned right at the first stop sign.

"Well, it's too late now." I chuckled. "Mrs. Taylor has officially left the building!"

"Did we really just do that?" Kendall asked me.

"We really did, huh? We's married nauw."

THE TAYLORS

When we each went into our spiritual fasts, neither of us had any idea that taking time away from romantic relationships to get clear about who we were apart from someone else, and what God wanted for our personal lives, would ultimately lead us to lasting love. But it didn't take either of us long to discover that by abstaining from mind-altering substances and avoiding the distractions that come from the opposite sex, we were finally able to get out of our own way and fully surrender to God so that He could lead our next moves. Of course, this wasn't easy and it won't surprise you to know that lots of people tell us that they don't want to go through that process. There were even moments in our own process that we considered aborting the mission! So, it is understandable that many people are like, "No, no, no, I don't have time for that. Been there, done that." We get it. But how do you know what kind of partner you need if you don't know who you are before you join to another? What we have learned is that once you become one with the Father, you develop a greater love for yourself and a solid love for self is the foundation that loving someone else should be built upon.

In the short time that we got to know each other before our marriage, we shared what may be viewed by some as the worst things about ourselves right from the jump. Most people would tell you not to do this in the spirit of the traditional first impression, especially in our society where most choose to hide behind filters instead of presenting their authentic selves. But we think it's important to be honest with the person you desire to receive honesty from in return. We learned that it's best not to try to play dress-up because in romance it's the comfort that can be found only in nakedness that breeds trust and loyalty. At some point you have to show the person your true ugly in order to determine if their eyes are equipped to capture your true beauty. You have to let them see the things you've been through, see all of your scars. That gives them the opportunity to decide whether they think you bring something of value to their life and whether they believe that they can add value to yours. Those moments of transparency turned out to be very important for us. We could each see who the other was and, after baring our souls, neither of us had anything left to hide. There was also nothing from our pasts that could ever be used against the potential that rested in our future. In the process we created verbal, emotional, and spiritual intimacy, which led to physical intimacy and a love that was full circle.

These steps and disciplines helped lead us to our fantasy "happily ever after." But by the time we married we had known each other for only three weeks. Little did we know that the real work of marriage had just started.

CHAPTER 2

KING AND QUEEN
Two Alphas, One Name

FANTASIA

Even though I'd spent seven months clearing out my spirit, I never expected love to happen to me so fast. When I came off-Broadway, I was enjoying the single life; I was cool with where I was. And then, BOOM!, I run into this bald-headed dude. But that wasn't my plan. I hadn't constantly been praying, "Lord, send me a man; Lord, send me my man," like I had in earlier years. I was embracing this new season of self-love and growing in the understanding of who I was as a woman at that time. With that comes a certain level of independence that I soon realized needed adjusting when we both agreed to become one.

So, when we got married, I said, "For better or worse, for richer or poorer." I stood before God and sealed this convenant. But when the ceremony was over and it was in our hands to uphold, some of my independence spilled over into "I want you to be what I want you to be." But Kendall wasn't trying to be that. I believe that the fear of being hurt can unknowingly convince us that we need to maintain control in order to feel protected, though we agreed to protect each other.

KENDALL

I had spent many years living alone. I had my daily routine and schedule that had become my comfort zone, and that intense level of structure convinced me that I, too, was in control. My strict and military-style type of rhythm didn't leave much room for her to fully express her personality and personal needs. I guess you can say that I wanted her to fit inside of my world, but she wasn't trying to be that either. Looking back, I now realize that though they were innocent in nature, these hidden expectations we were placing on each other were nothing more than our own insecurities. A major side effect of insecurity that is not dealt with is an unhealthy need for a sense of control.

FANTASIA

I didn't realize it at the time, but I walked into our marriage with my Timberland boots on. In every other relationship I'd been in, the man hadn't stepped up to be the man. So when Kendall came into my life, I was like, "You can't tell me how to do this right, so stop, because I have been doing this for fourteen years." If I could use an artist to describe who I was, it would probably be James Brown. I'd been watching movies and documentaries about him. He was a rebel and had to fight for his creative vision in an industry that was exploiting Black artists. He was like, "I'ma fight; it's gonna be mine; play it like I say play it; I want it to sound like this; nobody's gonna take nothing that belongs to me." Maybe you came to one of my shows during this time. If so, you saw me sing a lot of his music. At the end I would come out with a cape on and close with "Sleeping with the One I Love." People loved it—the men, in particular, would think it was crazy good! But while my audiences were enjoying good music that took them back in time, I wasn't singing about it just because I liked it; I was also in that place personally, businesswise, and creatively.

The fight I was in with the music industry was showing up in my life and my music. I was angry about how the industry had taken advantage of me. I was just nineteen when I won *Idol* and I was both prepared and not prepared. Until then, I had been singing in churches and weddings. Singing was my thing, hands down. As a performer, I had trained myself to please everybody. I knew nothin' about nothin' other than I liked to sing: just give me the mic and we can do it.

After winning sixty-four million votes, from the very beginning, I was poppin'. I was traveling the world, and everyone knew me. I had a jeans line, I had a lipstick line with MAC, a *New York Times* best-selling book, and I was selling all kinds of records.

But I was gullible, and I have this big heart, and I was a people pleaser. I'm a Southern girl. When I like you, I like you, I love you, and I trust you. I trusted anybody who came into my life. So I went in full-speed ahead like, "I love you guys. Oh, thank you so much for taking care of me. I know you got my back." So while my gift was ready for prime time, I was not ready for the business side of things. I did not know how the industry worked. I did not know who the good lawyers were and who the good accountants were. After I won *Idol*, my contract automatically assigned me to a big management company. I didn't have control over my money; I didn't have control over my account; therefore, I also didn't have control over my own success. I didn't know how much was coming in; I didn't know how much was going out.

It turns out that nobody had my back. I was topping the charts but wasn't bringing any of that money home. I didn't know that if you don't write the songs, you don't get paid when they get played on the radio. I didn't know I wouldn't earn anything from millions of my album sales. My contracts were set up so that I got paid from the stage only, based on my performances, which meant that I had to be a workaholic. I was gone away from my family—and from my little daughter, Zion—for way too long. People were prostituting my gift. I was just a money machine. I was exhausted because I was working so much but the money wasn't coming home. It was like, "Oh, you gotta keep working." Years later, I even learned many people in the circles around me were taking advantage of me. Just to give you an example, money that was being deducted for my taxes wasn't being sent to the IRS. Plus, some members of my band and crew were being paid in cash and I was left to settle their taxes that were owed. After everyone else got their royalties, commissions, and fees, I would get whatever was left, if anything.

One day, I had been on the road for what felt like forever and had finally made it back home. But when I went to order a pizza, my debit card was declined. I was like, "Hold up, I don't have any money in the bank?!"

I'll never forget the day that an older and more experienced R & B singer told me, "You need to check your stuff. I think they're brown-bagging you."

I was like, "What is that?"

"I think money's changing hands under the table," he said.

He was right. I ended up owing more than $1 million in taxes. I was like, "Hold up!" I lost the house I had bought for me and my family, and the embarrassment from the public ridicule was just as painful. I was exhausted and had to start all over. It was humiliating as well as devastating! Then some of the people around me and the media turned me into a national joke.

Even though a decade had passed since I won *Idol*—and even though I had made changes in my management—there were still a lot of wrong people in my life professionally. I knew it, but I didn't know how to solve it. So, when I met Ken, I was watching lots of documentaries about artists who had gone through the same things I was experiencing. All sorts of oldies-but-goodies about how so many of them went through dark times, depression, drugs, and alcohol; being cheated out of their money; being cheated out of their records; bad relationships—you have heard the stories before.

On top of that, the industry didn't know what to do with me creatively. When I was growing up, my family listened to all kinds of music, but the industry kept me trapped in the box of R & B. I do sing soul music and I love it. But I also sing gospel; I sing rock; I've sung with the Nashville Symphony orchestra; I sing country. I've even performed in Italian with the legendary opera singer Andrea Bocelli. You can't just squeeze me into one category, but that is what the industry kept trying to do.

So, when I met Ken, I was in the mode of "I'm gonna fight and I'm gonna fight hard; I'm gonna get what I want; I'm gonna get what I need in this business; they're going to respect me." I saw this very same level of passion and determination in Kendall as he began to share more and more of his personal story. He, too, had used his gifts to accomplish the impossible. He, too, had others who worked even harder to take it from him. We knew that we both had something special between us but were still trying to figure out exactly how to bring these two forces together under one roof.

KENDALL

The problems we encountered weren't all about her. I was still trying to establish myself personally and professionally. In 2007, when I got locked up for four months out of state, that became a turning point for me. I'd grown up in the church; my mother had tried to raise me in the right way. But missing a father, I did what a lot of young men do and looked for affirmation in the streets.

Anytime that I had previously been arrested in North Carolina, I would immediately make bail, but this time bail was not an option. Having to sit down forced me to stop drinking, getting high, and running from my weaknesses. While I was locked up, I returned to the Bible. But this time, I returned with an open and pure heart, meaning that I had finally reached a breaking point of humility within myself. I fasted; I read; I studied; I even led Bible study in my cell; I had a routine; I worked out; I stopped cussing. For years I'd struggled within myself about selling drugs. I didn't really want to sell them; I just didn't know how to live the life I envisioned for myself within the constraints that having felonies puts on you. But one day after wrestling with God for hours as I sat on the floor of my jail cell, I overcame that fear and gave my life to Christ.

It began when I noticed a brother in my cell block who never came out of his cell much. Anytime that I would walk by he would have his head down and nose glued to various books that were all spread across his tiny desk. One day I asked, "Yo, Mike, what are you studying?"

"Carolina, what's good? I'm seeking God, brother. Focused on the Most High."

For me, it was less about what he was doing than the way he was doing it. His consistency and discipline were what I was drawn to and respected most.

"You familiar with the Scriptures?" he asked me.

"Facts, but I'm clear there is more than what I'm catching from them."

"Well, if you're serious, meet me in the morn out in the open area after the five a.m. head count and we can get it in," Mike offered.

"Say less!"

I sat that entire evening excited about the following morning. I hungered and thirsted for something more and I felt that if I could find it in that dark and hopeless place, then my life could surely benefit from it in the outside world. So, at 5:00 a.m. sharp, Mike and I sat at the table and wasted no time regarding our mission.

"Psalms is a book of praise, brother," Mike explained. "These Scriptures unveil how great men worship and reverence our Father. Proverbs is a book of wisdom that we can lean on as we navigate the temptations of this world. Now, when we begin in Genesis..."

"Mike, pack up all your belongings; you're being shipped out!" a corrections officer stated through the intercom.

What! God, are You serious? I was frozen in disbelief, wondering why Mike was being shipped out now. Why not a week ago, or a week from now? I didn't understand. We both dapped and hugged and then I sat alone in the open area while he packed his few personal items and walked out of the cell block. Again, I found myself alone. I dropped my head and poured my heart out to God like I never had before. I couldn't control the tears that I normally was conditioned to suppress. I didn't care that I was in a jail environment; I no longer cared what those who may have heard or saw would think of me; I didn't care about anything other than feeling God's presence. And it was in this place, of being stripped of all the worldly materials and the validation that came from the streets and the opinions of others that had secretly dictated my identity, that God reintroduced Himself to me. Immediately I felt a powerful light surrounding me and warmth that was not of this world, a comfort of protection that I had not felt since I was a child and a peace that truly surpassed my present understanding.

"Father, You know the contents of my heart and how they don't reflect the actions and behaviors I have demonstrated. I am unsure of who I am anymore and what my purpose is in this world, but if You promise to walk with me, I will let go of all the things I have attached myself to and surrender to You. I will face whatever time and sentence they give me; just don't take Your presence that I feel in this moment away from me!"

At one point, I remember calling my mom.

"How are you doing? Do you need anything?" she asked me.

"No, ma'am, I'm in the best place of my life," I told her. "I'm in a dope place and for now, this is where I need to be."

Being in jail or prison has many negative effects on an individual's mental and physical health, as well as their ability to get an education or a job that allows them to do more than scrape by. It impacts children and families, because though one man gets sentenced, the entire family ends up doing time. But for me it forced me to focus on myself and gave me the opportunity to practice my gift of leadership where the followers were hopeless, resources were minimal, and lower expectations could not be found.[1]

When I got out, I knew God was giving me another chance. And at first, I just wanted to survive, get an apartment, and be a better father to my son—to just pay for my sins and move on. But by then I had three felonies. I was terrified of living my life inside the limitations that having a felony record creates. I felt like I had no options. I knew that I had more potential than to be confined to a menial job for the rest of my life, or to struggle to get housing, or not to have a passport, to be unable to vote, not to be legally able to carry a gun, and some of the other consequences of having a felony on your record.[2] So I wrestled and wrestled with God until I finally surrendered and agreed to live an honorable life, even though I had no idea

---

1. Prison Policy Initiative, https://www.prisonpolicy.org/blog/2021/05/13/mentalhealthimpacts/.
2. GTCadmin, "The Impact of a Felony Conviction," May 8, 2018, Halscott Megaro, https://www.appealslawgroup.com/the-impact-of-a-felony-conviction/.

how to do it inside those restrictions. So, for eighteen months, I did the only things I could think of to do: I worked a grueling schedule, focused on my personal and spiritual development, and I tried to build my relationships with God and my son.

As I surrendered to God's will, He opened up a path that allowed me to redeem myself righteously. Using some of the skills I'd honed legally over the years working in restaurants and retail, and some that I'd honed illegally as an entrepreneur in the streets, I hustled. In just eighteen months, I worked my way from making $7.25 an hour doing package fulfillment in a warehouse to building a transportation and logistics company that was grossing more than $500,000 a year in revenues and providing opportunities for ex-felons and other guys with backgrounds like mine.

Along the way, an older businessman who'd seen how I'd leveraged an opportunity and knew that he'd be retiring invited me to help him build his business in exchange for 49 percent ownership of his company if I could bring in $1 million in new revenue. This man began to introduce me to his networks, and from there it was just a matter of playing chess. To fulfill my end of the bargain, within six months I closed $1 million of new business. I found my rhythm and began closing contracts back-to-back, building partnerships and becoming influential in my region by being the businessman I always knew I could be.

All of this was still unfolding when my wife and I met in 2014; plus, I was still on probation at the time. Imagine that—I owned a multimillion-dollar company and couldn't legally secure an apartment in my own name. That's why I still saw myself as a man who was rebuilding his life and potentially not prepared to face the task of scripturally leading a woman, even more so one as powerful and famous as my wife. So, a part of me wasn't quite sure why Fantasia was so into me. She was so successful, at first sometimes I'd wonder,

What do I have to offer? Why is she interested in an ex-con-turned-businessman who is still living under the radar? Back then if you googled my name, several of my mug shots would still come up. But early in our relationship, she would not give up on me. She kept speaking to the King in me, and that felt dope, though I wasn't able to see yet what God was putting together between the two of us.

FANTASIA

I loved Ken and believed in him. He'd tell me about some of the stories from his past and I couldn't imagine them happening to the man sitting before me. (I was green. I didn't know anything about jail or the streets or that kind of thing.)

He'd talk about some of the limitations having felonies created and I would respond by saying, "I carry a lot of things, too, Ken, but look at me; God can do all things and you know that!"

KENDALL

Sometimes I'd tell her, "I don't think you understand, I can't, with the type of past that I have," do this thing or that thing, and she would say, "Yes, you can!"

She kept coming back and being loving and encouraging toward me. Her words compelled me to take greater risks than I would normally take on my own because it's a tremendous challenge operating in that level of faith when you are walking alone.

FANTASIA

Maybe I felt so positive about Ken's future because I had overcome so many of the negative and humiliating things that some people had said about me at different points in my life—that I would never amount to anything; that I'd ruined my life by getting pregnant during my teens; that I was illiterate; that I was a homewrecker; that

I'd been financially irresponsible. Yet here I was—a living testimony! So, with Ken I was like, "No, we're not gonna stand for that!"

But one day at about the three-month mark, the haze of romance disappeared, and we were just sitting in the room looking at each other like, "We really did this."

That's when the work began.

Trauma Drama

KENDALL

Whenever you bring two people together, you will always run into differences you have to work out. There are your lifestyles—from your eating habits, to what time you go to bed, to how you like your clothes folded, and things like that. You've got your bills, your credit scores, college debt, credit card debt, budgeting, spending habits, and other types of money-management issues. There's how to divvy up chores and other household responsibilities when two people have demanding jobs and busy lives. All sorts of stuff comes up in terms of in-laws and each other's families. The list of situations that you suddenly have to figure out can seem endless. In our case, these types of issues got amped up because we got married so soon and were each such a powerhouse in our own right. But as rocky as things got, our commitment helped us to make it through.

Whether you hit a rough patch at the beginning of your relationship or run into life and relationship challenges further down the line, you will experience them. We see lots of people quit as soon as they encounter marital turbulence. But we've found that you can get to a new season of deeper love if you dig into your commitment to each other, so you don't give up before you get to the other side of the problems. But for us to get over that hump, we had to set our egos aside, humble ourselves, and learn to be vulnerable. We had to realize that we can still be at war with the world around us and not be at war with each other. This required us to be intentional because outside the confines of our home, we were both seen as a king and a queen. We both called the shots and didn't answer to anyone else. We had to choose to lay those crowns aside for our marriage and to commit to leaving our titles and accolades at the front door before we entered. This opened the door for us to come into agreement with each other. As we practiced submitting our individual egos for the good of our relationship, we began to discover that we could accomplish things together that we couldn't do as individuals. We started caring less about the accolades we would receive from the world and more for the respect and admiration that we supplied to each other. When we started laying down our individual crowns, we began to view our partner as our crown and our family as our crown. Besides, only the crown that God gives you is everlasting.

FANTASIA

We both had issues that we needed to work on. But looking back I think that most of the problem was me.

Even though I'd fasted for seven months in New York, one thing I didn't do was get rid of my trauma and generational curses, which I'll tell you more about in chapter 4. For now, let's just say that I've witnessed firsthand how men can operate without respecting women—cheating, not caring, and so on. Needless to say, I didn't want that to be me. I got super scared about acknowledging that Ken really loved me and would be there for me. I became overprotective of myself.

I also supported a lot of people financially until I accepted that love and respect should not come with a price tag. But now that I had found love and wasn't the old unhappy Fantasia anymore, I began to make different decisions concerning money, and the result was that people began to separate themselves from me. To this day I am still not on speaking terms with certain ones who once were inseparable. At times I would silently wonder to myself, *How am I going to build a family when I come from so much brokenness?*

KENDALL

Brokenness began to reveal itself on both sides. She was supporting people financially; I was supporting people financially. People were asking her for money; they were asking me for money.

FANTASIA

I have also been in some very bad and even verbally and physically abusive relationships. My life growing up was not a fairy tale.

Now that I was married, all sorts of trauma and hurt that I thought my time of fasting had cleansed began to regurgitate and bubble up. Until then, I'd thought that if I just found the right person, it would wash away my pain; it would wash away my bad memories.

I would start acting out, like, "You do not know what I have been through." Or, "Do not talk to me anymore." Or, "You remind me of [something or someone negative] from my past."

I made him constantly prove that he loved me. Sometimes I would stay out until 5:00 a.m. posting things on social media, but then I wouldn't always respond to his texts. I used my trauma and experiences that I'd gone through before as an excuse. It was like I had him on trial. Eventually he got burned out.

On top of that, I have another generational curse—the power of the tongue. Back then, I was a pop-off, a firecracker—*pow, pow, pow, pow!*

KENDALL

My wife and I, we both had trauma. From shoot-outs that I'd experienced as a teenager and adult, which left me with untreated

PTSD, I've carried anxiety for much of my life. Back then, I was always jumpy and intense; I took short breaths, and my shoulders would be so tense. It hadn't occurred to us that our traumas would manifest and intensify inside the incubator of our marriage.

On top of our traumas bubbling up, before I got married, I came from relationships where I always wanted things my way. If it was not my way, I was out—I was that guy. I knew the logistics of love, what Valentine's Day and birthdays meant, that I was not supposed to talk to other girls, and that kind of thing. I would think about how a woman looked and what I desired to receive from the relationship, but before I knew my wife, I didn't really understand love as God originally designed it. Today, I can look back and see how much I candy-coated my selfishness under smiles and sweet words filled with manipulation. I brought that selfish expectation into our marriage. So, a big piece of the man I have become is because of the way she shouldered my negativity, my selfish ways, my shortsightedness through her forgiveness and the manner in which she loved me became the blueprint I used to properly love her in return.

Also, in the beginning of our marriage our lifestyles clashed. I would leave early in the morning to go to work. I would crash by eight or nine o'clock because I had to get up at five in the morning. She is an artist, so she would be up all night.

FANTASIA

I was also always on the road all week. I had almost no days off. I was doing walk-throughs, shows, working to help get out of a financial hole. My feet were completely tired. I was blowing my knees out. My vocals were tired. I missed my children. In the industry, I was surrounded by wolves in sheep's clothing. But I couldn't let the public know. I was always posting happy pictures even when I was feeling sad. Then, Kendall and I entered a stage where we got into this spirit of competition, where nobody could lead, nobody could follow, nobody could surrender, nobody could submit. We had both found incredible success in our own right, wearing our own crowns, and we had our egos cocked back and ready to prove it.

I had my company, he had his company, and our businesses were separate. We were like, "I have been doing it like this"; or, "I rock this way"; or, "I have been making millions." We started competing and tearing each other down. It was like I didn't understand his crown and he didn't understand mine. We went through a lot of nights where we were not talking. Where I was in the front of the tour bus and he was in the back of the bus, and at times it was the same at home. It almost pushed us apart to where we were going to end up independent of each other, and in marriage that road leads only to divorce. We kept bumping heads because we were both trying to bring our separate ideals, our separate crowns, to spaces where unity and compromise are supposed to be found instead.

FANTASIA

Before I went on my fast, I used to love me some prosecco and orange juice, a good mimosa. In my younger days, I could drink to the point where people would be like, "How many shots did you have and you are still walking?" For me, I was used to it: "This is how we do it in my circles." Get so drunk you pass out; you black out. Go hard or go home.

KENDALL

I never drink more than two drinks, a clean pour. My security rests in maintaining a level head, so I protect it at all times and at all costs.

FANTASIA

As all those bad memories bubbled up, I started drinking again, really heavy. My drinking became a thing. My mother used to warn me, "Watch how much you drink. Your grandfather had a problem."

"Mom, I am not him," I would tell her.

"Why do you have to drink so much?" she would ask, seeing the way I was going.

When I would drink I would get angry, very angry, fighting angry, embarrassing-him angry. We would throw a party and invite people over and end up arguing. I would wake up the next morning like, "Oh my God, what happened? What did I do?"

Ken, he was not used to that.

One time after an argument, I'd gone to Vegas without him. You know how you post pictures where you look okay, fine, happy even though you're not? Well, I was stunting and putting on a big front, posting pictures of me laughing even though on the inside I was sad. Ken was back in Charlotte watching it all unfold on Instagram.

KENDALL

All of this celebrity stuff was new to me. It's not the world I come from. Privacy is and always will be important to me, and I began to feel that this world was outside of my understanding and ability to lead.

FANTASIA

At one point I called home to talk to my mom. She told me that Ken had packed everything he had in a work van and left.

"He didn't leave not one thing behind," my mom told me.

When I got home from Vegas, he was still gone. I was mad and embarrassed, but still I refused to reach out to him. When my silence didn't get the reaction I wanted, I put my wedding rings on the nightstand, took a picture, posted it to Instagram, and said, "It's over."

KENDALL

I was at the job when my employee was like, "Have you seen what she put on Instagram?" That is the point when I put my shell back up, reaching out for that sense of control.

I'd built my business under the radar to protect myself. Now I could see that she had the power to destroy everything I'd built with just a swipe of her celebrity sword. Suddenly, I'd go to networking events and my conversations with customers were no longer strictly about business. They were, "What happened? What happened? Are you okay?"

It was too much.

Plus, the public loves and adores her; at that time, I was just a felon with no celebrity equity in their eyes. Someone could annihilate me just because it's good publicity. Millions of dollars of contracts were on the line. I had to do damage control to protect my name and what I'd built. So, I told my partner to take my name off the company as CEO; I'd just be president. There was way too much negative attention.

Eating Humble Pie

FANTASIA

When Kendall moved out, I felt like God was checking me for my behavior. I tried to reach out to him, but he had blocked me on everything. I couldn't call; I couldn't email him; I couldn't hear his voice; I couldn't get in touch.

Nothing.

Like, it was over-over.

(Do not make a Leo mad, honey!)

I had pushed Ken away; now I was being tested. Every day seemed like it went on forever. One day turned into two; then it was one week; then one month; then two. Our breakup just went on and on. I had a lot of sleepless nights.

It wasn't until I lost my husband that I started looking at myself in the mirror. I realized that I was carrying a monster that had been destroying my true desire for happiness and I had to let it go. Even though I was wanting love, I'd put a shield around my heart. I grew up seeing so many women get played and taken advantage of that I believed I had to operate in a certain way to keep myself protected.

But now I was like, "No, 'Tasia, that's bs; that's a game."

I had to be honest with myself and say, "You know what? I did pick this behavior up from [such and such experience], or [such and such person] in my life."

I knew that there were some things that I needed to change, so I decided to do a Daniel fast, where you eat only plant-based foods for forty days as an act of worship and sacrifice. It was my first time doing it, so it was hard. But spiritually it ended up being the best fast ever.

I would ask God, "Speak, Lord; please speak to me."

I was already a dreamer—I keep track of my dreams and read about what's in them for spiritual guidance. During my fast, my dreams were amazing! God was getting me into shape by showing me all sorts of things I had to let go of. I realized the bottle couldn't help me. Champagne and wine weren't even numbing my pain anymore. God was like, "Okay, you had your seven months in New York. You were doing okay until you were tested. Now all your fear is trying to take over your faith." That was the first time I realized that Kendall would be my king and that God had brought him into my life for a reason. It was only after I released all of my pains and fears over to

God in His love that I could be open to receiving the love God was sending to me through Kendall. I needed to go back to get him.

KENDALL

While we were apart, things were very difficult on my end too.

Right around the time my wife and I met, the situation changed between me and my business mentor and partner. To make a long story short, after I turned our company profitable, we started having all kinds of problems with the transition toward me taking full control. The hours I was working were insane. I was under an incredible amount of stress.

FANTASIA

Then things went from bad to worse. I lost my grandmother unexpectedly to a massive heart attack. This was my mother's mother, who had helped raise me throughout my whole entire life. She had met Kendall just one time, but she knew he was special and special to me.

"You know you're special to God," she had said when she saw him.

Now I was even more heartbroken 'cause he'd left.

Ken had been my protector; he calmed me; he made me feel safer. So, when my mom called to tell me my grandmother had passed, I knew I had to find him. I tried to call but he wouldn't pick up, so I sent him an email to tell him what had happened and that I was planning her funeral and wanted him to come. He replied.

KENDALL

When she contacted me, I was laid up and literally could not walk. I had bulging disks in my back from a freak accident. I had been getting back-to-back cortisone shots and was considering surgery. So

I told my wife, "I cannot come to the funeral. I cannot walk; I cannot sit up. But I will get somebody to drive me to High Point, and I can lie in a bed in the hotel, just so I can be close to you."

FANTASIA

That hit a nerve. I was used to him giving me what I wanted. I was like, "Who is this person?" As you can tell, I was being selfish. Even though his back was down, I was still like, "I need you to get here." But on the day of the funeral, he couldn't make it.

These were dark times for both of us. We didn't know this back then because we had just met, but looking back on things, I believe something spiritual was going on. Today we know that our marriage is such a powerful spiritual connection that when we are at odds, both of us get physically sick. We have learned that we were joined by God to fight together and never against each other. When we fight together, there is nothing that we have not been able to overcome and defeat, but when we are against one another we are unable to accomplish even the most basic tasks in our day-to-day lives. When we cast our crowns before the throne of God as we are commanded, that leaves no room for personal egos and selfishness to rule and reign in our marriage.

There was this song, a gospel song titled "Never Wanna Let You Go" by the Walls Group, that I'd play every day along with Mahalia Jackson, that reminded me of my grandmother. The song also reminded me of Ken.

In the days after my grandmother's funeral, I would go to God and say, "God, teach me how to be a good wife to him." And "God, I cannot talk to him about [this and that], but I am coming to You because You are his Father. I am coming to You because You are his Creator."

During that time, God deepened my understanding of humility.

I reached the point where I was like, "Okay, God, I'll do whatever it takes. I don't know what's necessary, but I'm gonna need You to help me."

Ken likes chocolate, so that was the same as roses to me. One day I got in my truck and drove to the grocery store and picked up his favorite sweets and one of those chocolate arrangements where they make little flowers out of candy bars. Then I drove to his job. I had "Never Wanna Let You Go" blasting. I was scared. He might reject me. He might play me in front of all the people who worked for him.

I sat in the car praying and counting to ten a couple of times to build up my courage. Then I swallowed my pride and went inside, hoping to get my man.

"Please tell Kendall that I am here," I said to the receptionist, my knees knocking and my heart racing as fast as Tech N9ne rhymes.

When she let me in, I set the candy on his desk. I don't know exactly what I said; God spoke through me. It was something like, "I can't do this; I can't live like this; I need you in my life. I will do whatever it takes to earn your trust again. We can go as slow as you want to go. We do not have to stay the night together tonight. We do not have to kiss. We can just become friends again. Give me that chance to start over. I will do whatever I need to do, I promise."

KENDALL

When my admin told me that my wife was here to see me, my heart jumped through the roof. But she had just put me through a lot of drama, so I tried to keep my emotions in check.

As she apologized to me, I was thinking to myself, *She is a celebrity and yet she walked in and humbled herself. She could have chosen to behave the total opposite way.*

I knew there had been times she'd forgiven me for my ignorance and stupid stuff, so I did not feel like being anything other than the comforter she needed me to be and God required of me. She came to me and showed me that nothing mattered more than us being together and working through everything that we had going on, relentlessly. I was like, "If she loves me that much that she doesn't care about what she has going on, with her grandmother passing, then I am never going to let those kinds of things come between us either." Plus, she used the cheat code and took advantage of my sweet tooth; she had Kit Kats. What was I supposed to do? I couldn't resist.

My wife cast her crown, her ego, her talent aside. So, in that moment I was moved and inspired to do the same.

FANTASIA

The afternoon that I put down my crown, that was the day I became his Queen. My husband came back home. It had been the longest three months of my life.

The Bridge Called Commitment

KENDALL

At this point, we had to erase all the old ways that we had been operating. We had a long way to go. Everything that happened had come at a cost. I didn't come back the same way I left.

People in my close network would be like, "Are you sure about this?" They were protective of me just like people are protective of her. But I threw that to the wind because my wife and I had shared something I hoped that we'd reclaim.

I came back a different dude. I hesitated in the beginning. I'd seen the power of fame wielded in a way that could have hurt me even worse than it did. I didn't feel safe. I didn't trust her. I'd gotten a taste of, "I have a lightsaber; you could be destroyed!"

While God was rebuilding her, some of the same behavior I'd

experienced then came out of me. I wasn't patient or understanding. The sense of security that had made me jump and marry her was gone. In the beginning, I'd always been calm on some Zen, Buddha, Gandhi type of flow; I don't like drama. Now that I was coming back, I felt very unsure, unstable. I would threaten, I would curse—anything might fly out of my mouth.

So, though I started coming back, I was like, "Let me apply pressure and let me see if you'll stay with me." And my pressure is pressure. Serious pressure. Looking back, I realize that it was immature and unmanly of me to communicate forgiveness verbally yet withhold it in my actions and demonstration of a loving leader.

For a while we went back and forth. Eventually, we ran out of steam. We reached a point where we were forced to ask ourselves, "Are we gonna walk out the Scriptures and learn how to reach agreement so that each of us can have a true helpmate who is understanding at all times and a balanced, wholesome, healthy, forward-moving relationship—or are we going to stay stuck inside our egos and block our own blessings?"

At that point it was like, "Let's get focused and go back to the beginning." Could we cross back over that dusty, trusty bridge called commitment—the bridge to our next season we both knew that we needed to cross?

Casting Down Our Crowns

KENDALL

God gives you a crown that man cannot see. That is your spiritual crown. You have a spiritual crown and a worldly crown. Your worldly crown consists of the jobs, titles, and credentials that are bestowed on you out in society. Designer labels, the car you drive, the neighborhood you live in, the size of your office, the title on the door or your badge, the certificate hanging on the wall, and other things that give you status—those are all worldly things. Things of the world; they come and go. But if you want to take your relationship and your life to the next level, we want you to make the decision that you will not wear your worldly crown in the crib.

Your spiritual crown outlasts your worldly crown; in fact, it is everlasting.[3] My worldly crown is adorned with the jewels of expectations and the value others place on me. This crown is temporary and will slowly fade with time and age. However, my spiritual crown is adorned with jewels of character and righteous conduct that reflect the gift of God's salvation. No one can redefine who God declares I am and the value He has placed on my life. I can fully believe in this spiritual crown because the One who placed it on my head is eternally trustworthy. So, how does a man receive his own crown that can't be taken away? You walk in the opposite direction of most men in this world and set your sights on the direction in which Christ walked. You open the door to receiving that crown by surrendering your will and objectives over to His leadership, which will purify and recondition yours. Then, by demonstrating the strong mental, emotional, and moral character that promotes true strength and integrity, you can begin to rebuild things that you once constructed with stones of selfishness and floor plans of immaturity. Think of your integrity, honesty, intentions, work ethic, determination, and endurance as the architectural blueprint of your character. The way you do things, the way you posture yourself, the way you respond to other people, the way you conduct yourself as a man (or woman)—these characteristics give you a divine strength that is worthy of respect. Men unwilling to do this internal work, which is required for lasting transformation, often resort to adorning themselves outwardly with

---

3. BibleStudy.org, "What Do Crowns Symbolize?," https://www.biblestudy.org/question /crowns-in-the-bible.html.

trinkets, hoping to mask the faulty foundations of their true identity lying underneath.

Jobs and material possessions don't last. But with your spiritual crown, it doesn't matter what happens to you—you can get locked up like I did or have a million-dollar tax bill like my wife had—no one can take your spiritual character away. As a matter of fact, the trials and difficulties that we undergo often give us the chance to make our character stronger. You cannot get a title like JD, MD, or PhD without having to go through seasons of study, sacrifice, testing, and approval. You should not get the title of pastor, preacher, prophet, or bishop without having gone through seasons and trials in the fiery furnace that qualifies you. The same thing is true when you earn your spiritual crown. Have you suffered? Have you been broken down and allowed God to build you up again? And now that you are on that mountain of redemption, are you building up others? That is the true mark of character. That is a heavy and weighty crown. When you are living a righteous life, your character becomes your spiritual crown, which is eternal and comes with authority and power.

We live in a world where people focus on superficial things, and we often hide behind our accolades and money, as my wife and I did early in our marriage. Oftentimes couples wear their crowns around their home. Sometimes we put them on when we're losing a fight, when our character is being cross-examined, or when our partner is addressing our weaknesses and the chinks in our armor. Instead of just humbling ourselves and saying, "I was wrong; you are correct," sometimes we say, "No, I am a doctor; I have a master's degree; you do not know anything." But a worldly crown should merely enhance your character, not be the source of it. It should bring value and help you elevate and edify the person you are already on the path to becoming, but should not define who you are.

Earthly crowns also come attached with spiritual responsibilities.

Our gifts, talents, skills, and abilities come from heaven. There is no greater demonstration of power than to be in possession of your gift and consciously choose not to showcase it for worldly attention and accolades, but to choose to demonstrate humility instead. Psalm 8:5 states, "You have made them a little lower than the angels and crowned them with glory and honor." One of the most important stages of our marriage took place when my Queen and I realized that we did not want to wear our worldly crowns in our castle.

FANTASIA

I've noticed that sometimes as we walk around demonstrating our shabby character, we say, "Jesus, I am waiting on You," then wonder why nothing in our lives is changing. Nothing is changing because our character is not changing. Change your character and you'll change how life responds to you. In life, you can't afford to get stuck in one place. You have to grow in life and you have to grow in your marriage. As you do that, you get to experience more of life's abundance.

When Kendall and I entered into our marriage, we had no idea how important humility would be. When we talk about being humble, we're not talking about being lowly, weak, a punk, or some other derogatory word. It just means you understand that you don't know everything and you're not perfect. You aren't arrogant. You understand and embrace the fact that even in all you've accomplished, it was less about you and more about God working through you to manifest those great things that you've been privileged to be a part of.

Kendall and I wanted our marriage to be rooted and founded in Christ, but we had to figure out how to make that work. One thing that turned out to be important for me was developing a better understanding of who I am. When God checked me, He reminded me that my character was not about gold records, where I debuted on a chart, or whether I sold more albums than another artist— other things I was thinking about at the time. Kendall taught me that, biblically, I am a queen. He started calling me Queen. Every text message from him ended with Queen, Queen, Queen, Queen. At first, it felt awkward.

KENDALL

Calling my wife Queen was about three things: One, when you're in a relationship with a woman who has had men before you and has been called by every pet name imaginable, how does she recognize and distinguish my call from all others? Two, if I don't call her Queen, I'm also not demonstrating my faith that God has made me a king on earth. So calling her Queen reinforces what I am and keeps me in a kingly posture. And, three, Fantasia is my wife's name and it's her stage name; it's how the world knows her. Calling her my Queen is just between us.

FANTASIA

My King helped me start walking into a higher vision of myself as a woman. Before him, I'd never texted anyone or any of my friends, "Hey, Queen, how are you?" I did not start calling women Queen until he started calling me Queen. But now I believe that we all should know who we are. When I talk to my friends, I call them queens.

I did not call him King right off the bat. I was not used to that, real talk. But as we grew, we started going back and forth. I started to call him King and he constantly calls me Queen. I see him as a man with vision, dreams, and goals. I see the king in him; it's embedded in him and instead of trying to fix him, I've learned to call it out of him. We remind each other on the daily.

KENDALL

To get to the type of marriage that I wanted to experience, I've had to kill my ego, my pride, and my selfishness.

Before I met my wife, I had been inconsiderate in relationships. You go back and ask my last ten exes and they will probably say, "He was a decent guy. He was a monster. He was a savage. He was an I-do-not-know." But when you meet the right woman, her love activates things in you that you did not know even existed. Suddenly, I had met my match. I could not figure out why she loved me so much, and it caused me to change. I wanted to learn how to love.

At first, I read all the books and watched the movies, but I was unable to convert what I was learning into action. That's partly because I had never humbled myself to sit back to study, observe, investigate, and interview the heart of a woman before. I began to consider, What did she need from me? What did she like? What was the best way to communicate with her? I had to ask her, practice, ask for feedback, and learn.

It took me a minute to understand that loving my wife meant dying to myself—killing off unhelpful parts of my personality.

I had to break my old patterns. To give you an example, I could not just sit in my office or leave all day and expect our disagreements to fix themselves the way I had in other relationships. I had to humble myself and apologize. I had to learn how to say, "I did not have to do that."

There are still these rare times when we are in separate rooms and not talking, and I have to overcome my ego in order to kill the negative thoughts and feelings I'm having that prevent me from leading. Because what I feel in any given moment is not more important than the love we create together when we are operating in agreement.

FANTASIA

You can put Kendall in a room with anyone, and by the time they leave they wanna be his best friend; they wanna do business with him. Whether it's musicians or corporate types, he has the gift of being able to blend into any scenario like a chameleon.

KENDALL

On one day in question, we had deals on the table; millions of dollars; hiring and firing at stake. Back home after the meeting, we were in a disagreement, and I was coming at her and making my points with a very negative tone and approach. That's when she checked me.

FANTASIA

I told him, "You go into some of the biggest meetings, tackle some of the biggest deals, the biggest projects, and you always act respectful no matter how irate the people get. You are the one who controls the tempo. You do it with the most calm and elegant composure. You got self-control. Why can you not do that with me?"

KENDALL

I came back at her with what most of us come with—excuses: I do not care about them like that. I do not love them like that, yada yada.

FANTASIA

You don't speak to your clients like that. You will not talk to the mailman like that. You do not let your neighbor see your other side.

KENDALL

Boom! She was right. My answer wasn't sufficient. I had to humble myself and apologize and tell my wife that she was right; then I had to change my behavior. If you are going to wear the crown of a husband, then you have to carry the spiritual responsibilities that come with it. The Scriptures will always bear witness to your character as a man.

If we would learn to reach for our companion quicker than we reach for our worldly crown and allow that to become the habit, we'd find that worldly things start not to even matter. Spiritually, we know that the world cannot tear us down because we are not measuring ourselves by worldly things—whether cars or jewelry, this label or that name brand. I am not defined by Cartier. I am not defined by a Gucci belt. I am not defined by Nike kicks and neither is my wife. I can wear some OshKosh B'gosh and stand in God's grace and position and never be moved.

As you develop spiritually, not only does your character become your crown, but your companion becomes your crown; your love for your family becomes your crown; the way your children view you becomes your crown.

FANTASIA

Learning to humble ourselves was a really, really important skill that allowed us to get through our first set of challenges in our marriage. We had to work through our egos, our pride.

I also started being more conscious about leaving my accolades out on the road. I did not return into our home like, "I have been on the road, so cook your own food." No, I do not walk around with a glass of wine and evening wear with a million feathers—even though I would love to find a robe with some feathers on it. I come home from the road and after I am able to rejuvenate, I am back rocking in wife and mommy mode.

The Power of Agreement

FANTASIA

Once we began to realize how important it was to put our crowns down, we were able to experience just how much more powerful we became when we reached agreement as a couple. The Bible talks about how when two or three people are gathered in His name, God can get down into the relationship with them and help. We experience that. Often.

As a singer, when I think about coming together, I think about how important it is that everyone's voices blend and harmonize. Just as I learned musically from my father, you want to create a song where each voice and instrument has their own notes and their own pockets, but they complement one another. In a Broadway musical, the audience may have come to see the lead performers, but part of why they sound so good is the other cast members—the chorus and band or orchestra—who are backing them up. The writers, dancers, and choreographers; the costume department; the hair and makeup artists; the people who design and build the stage; the folks who do the lighting; the sound guys; and others behind the scenes. All those different parts of the performance have to come together and be coordinated so the show kills it and the audience goes home feeling inspired and like the show was worth their time and money. And while money is not exchanged in a marriage, or at least I hope it's not, our time invested, emotions, and providing a sense of security deserve a return of loyalty and happiness just the same.

KENDALL

As a businessman, when I consider what it takes for entities to come together, I immediately start thinking about acquisitions—

how two companies, two juggernauts, join in a merger. They come together not to compete with each other but to form an alliance that allows them to compete on a greater level out in the marketplace. So, they're careful to handle that merger and acquisition delicately. They go through every single line item to make sure that those things gel. If not, the new organization starts to become toxic on the inside. And when they take their eye off what they were supposed to be doing when they partnered, when there's too much clashing and friction inside it, the new organization loses.

My wife doesn't need to be Kendall. She doesn't need to think like me, speak like me, move like me, push like me. I don't need to feel the way she feels, or think the way she thinks, or speak the way she speaks. But we do need to find ways to gel in harmony so that we can accomplish the purpose for which God merged us together in marriage, being separate identities now consolidated into one.

FANTASIA

We all have to find our own notes and rhythms and pockets. I have to let him sing his song in his tone, his voice. Then we need to match each other. If I'm talking to you in Billie Holiday tones, I'm not expecting you to come back at me all James Brown. There are times when I help him out in an area by saying, "Maybe try this note." And he, on his end—with his genius, smarts, intelligence—he will come in and teach me some things that I can add to my stage presence that nobody else would ever think about.

From the beginning, Ken and I agreed that we'd join our bank accounts. We realize that not everybody does that, but we did. Money touches everything inside of a relationship, so financially, we wanted to start out moving in the same direction, together. Merging our money immediately challenged us to come into agreement about how much we were gonna spend. We had to agree what our priorities were, what we were gonna do, how we were gonna do it.

I know talking about budgeting might sound funny coming from a celebrity, but every dollar counts and many people in the public eye don't have as much money as you think. For most of my career, even though I was making lots of money for other people, I struggled. Even at the time when Ken and I met, I'd drive to my manager's house in my old car, and see him with two fancy cars, Versace this, Versace that, Louis Vuitton carpet. But I was constantly told, "You don't have it." (Just for the record, I'm not the only one. It's one of the reasons why you see so many artists going independent.)

I have been broke not once, but twice. The second time happened after we got married. It was critical for me to view money differently and that in turn changed the way in which I handle it.

KENDALL

We were constantly warring with our companies. They were outside of our marriage, but they impacted the inside of our marriage. Partners tried to make us bend to their agenda, dance to the beat of their drum. They wanted to dictate our worth, what we could do, what we would be paid. Because we were at war with the world, we constantly had to remind ourselves that we were not at war with each other.

FANTASIA

The situation put a lot of pressure on us. I was working so hard, and I would go back to the hotel room and fall on my knees exhausted. I had already overcome and paid the million-dollar tax bill, so I was just wiped out. I loved my gift and my fans, but I hated the industry because the money I was making still wasn't coming home. I would cry and be like, "When is this going to be over?"

I knew Ken had all these challenges going on in his job, so one day I said, "Babe, we can do bad by our self. You know how to make money and I know how to make money. I know my gift and I know you can run a business. Let's just go independent and just leave everybody behind."

KENDALL

So on my end, I offered to buy my partner out. That did not go as planned. That's a story I'll tell you more about later. For now, suffice it to say I ended up losing everything I had put into the business and was left with nothing.

When my wife and I got married, I had labored for years to rebuild my life and had created a multimillion-dollar company. Now, just a little over one year after meeting this powerful woman who was now my wife, my partner beat me for millions. It was like I had gone back to square one. I went through a period of serious depression. I didn't have much bounce-back. I was tired; I was embarrassed. It just seemed like this was the cycle of my life.

At another stage in my life, I might have responded differently than I did. I knew that I had every right to get back what was rightfully mine. But both of us knew that God don't like ugly, so we agreed to demonstrate character and continue to be who we are and let Him handle it. Romans 12:19 says, "Vengeance is mine; I will repay" (KJV). So even as difficult as it was, I took my hands off of it and let God take care of it. Trust us when we say we take no pleasure in this, but one year later, the company was out of business.

FANTASIA

A few years into our marriage, King and I decided to come together and start our own record label and go independent. Our company is called Rock Soul Entertainment. We also knew that Ken wanted to start Salute First, his business where he teaches men about leadership and character. When we were trying to get them off the ground, we were broke. I mean, broke-broke.

For date nights, we would make tuna or bologna sandwiches and go to the airport and just watch the airplanes take off. I thought it was romantic; I would be grinning from ear to ear. Then again, I'm a country girl; I'm down-to-earth.

KENDALL

As a result of having this experience, as a couple our faith and our power are not built on any material stuff. We literally built our marriage from the gutter. We dug our marriage out when we had nothing, so it wasn't contingent on success or fame or popularity or the ability to take a trip or hop over to an island.

FANTASIA

Going independent was a big decision and it taught us that one person's voice can't be bigger than the other's. As a couple in business together, we had to learn how to come to agreement on big issues and small ones. My ideas couldn't count for more than his and his couldn't count for more than mine. Both of our ideas and opinions had to matter.

KENDALL

We understand now that when you're married, God sees only one spirit man, and that is the two of us together; there is no separation. As a married couple, we are more powerful when we reach agreement. We've learned that when we get off balance, that's when the leeches can creep in. If two people are together and they do not agree, they do not have a vision; that is a division.

Queen and I, we are one body so we often go against the grain of the world to find ways to reach agreement. We do some things that are opposite of what the industry does, or society does, or the world does. We have to figure out how to be in this world but not of this world. That means we have had to do things like pull back the layers and say, "Okay, I am going to take off my CEO hat and you take off yours."

In the beginning I needed to ask, "What do you need as my wife? What do you need to feel fulfilled, to feel complete, to feel empowered, to feel in control—and how can I help you have that? I am going to take care of everything else." And she did the same. In the process I found my space inside of what we do together, especially since I am married to this powerful and gifted woman who also happens to be a celebrity.

FANTASIA

And even when Ken and I disagree, now we've been through so many things together that we know we will be victorious over it. Disagreements don't have to become arguments. We now see them as opportunities to gain a deeper understanding of each other and bring peace where the spirit of confusion is waiting to creep in.

Bishop T. D. Jakes talks about the importance of looking for a partner who has a great foundation. In our marriage, we each looked for and have found somebody who has a great character, a great foundation—and we are building on that. Rome was not built in a day. This house that we are sitting in was not built in a day. Relationships take time, especially if you want them to stand and to last.

The key is to not just say, "I give up; I throw in the towel!" We don't know everyone's situation, but from our perspective too many people are doing that too fast. In the days of the Bible, many of the characters never gave up. They walked by faith and allowed God to lead them, and that is what we believe we have got to do.

I tried out for *Idol* in Atlanta at the Georgia Dome. When we got there, there were people everywhere—more people than you see on TV. People had brought tents and sleeping bags and they were sleeping outside the stadium in them. We couldn't afford all that. You had to go inside and get a number. I had my lip pierced at the time. When I went in, there was this older man, maybe in his sixties, who was doing security. He saw my piercing and asked me why I had it. I told him I thought it was cute. He said, "You're beautiful. You're going to mess up your lip." So we just started talking and talking. We must have talked for an hour. When we came back the next morning to get in line, the doors were already closed. Me and my brother, who had come with me, were just like, "Wait a minute, you gotta let us in! I've been singing since I was five years old; this is the biggest moment; this is everything for me; people in High Point, North Carolina, raised money, rallied together to get me here." But no one would let us in, so we left. Our father told us to go back. I was like, "Go back for what?" So my brother and I go back and go to the other side of the building. We were just walking the grounds praying. Next thing you know, here comes the older man from the day before. He asked me how it went. I told him I couldn't get in. He told me, "Hold on." He returned with someone from the show, who let us in. I ended up being the last person who got to audition. That's one of the reasons I believe in angels to this day.

If Ken and I had given up back in the beginning of our marriage, we wouldn't be where we are today. There have been many times that one of us has emotionally closed and locked a door, but we would hear God say, "Go back," just like my father told us back then. And though we have had to learn to humble ourselves in our relationship to each other and we had to learn to be humble in the world when we lost everything, now our business is rocking and rolling and we sit in our dream home. There's not a day that I don't wake up and tell God

"Thank You"; there's not a day that I don't wake up and say, "Okay, now I can see why we had to lose everything; it was necessary." Now we appreciate things a bit more; we take good care of what has been restored to us; now we look at things more spiritually.

We are the King's kids. We were built to be victorious. We are not going to fail, but we have to be patient and allow God to do His thing. Victorious people were never meant to settle for normal. The hidden key to obtaining power in the kingdom opposite of this world is found in humility. So we humble ourselves and we work to reach agreement.

We have differences of opinion, but we are each other's ace. At the end of the day, I would rather walk into a room with Kendall than anybody else.

KENDALL

Agreement has never been more important to me than it is now, because I have reached a point of understanding that I do not want to and cannot do life on my own. There is no victory that will be sweet if we do not accomplish it together. It does not matter if she is doing another lipstick line or nail polish, I'll be figuring out how to get the cheapest products on the manufacturing floor and maximize distribution. If I am speaking around the country, she is giving me tips on how to make my presentation more creative and captivating. Our gifts have room for each other's so we can accomplish anything that we imagine possible.

FANTASIA

Ken has also made a place for me to come alongside him, as well. I do part of Salute First. There is no separation anymore. We have several businesses in our marriage and we agree to participate and contribute collectively across the board. We want to be in agreement not just in word but also in spirit, action, and deed.

THE TAYLORS

Many of us will experience times when love can't be found, and communication is difficult. We haven't always talked to each other kindly, or behaved in loving ways, or been willing to sacrifice. We've both been through a lot of pain and trauma, and we have taken some of it out on each other. We've each done things that the other could have left us for. We both have scars. It's been hard. We've had messy moments like everyone else.

That said, we have struggled our way through the early turbulence in our relationship. In the process we learned that we had to set down our egos, humble ourselves, and learn to be vulnerable with each other so we could learn how to love the other in a way that each of us could believe in and grow to trust. After we submitted our egos to what was good for the relationship, we discovered how much more power we had when we came into agreement with each other. Suddenly, we could accomplish things together that couldn't get done on our own. Now we know that if either or both of us can humble ourselves for long enough to come into agreement—if we can put down our individual crowns and experience our relationship with God, our partner, and our family as our crown—we can make it across the bridge of commitment and enter into our next season.

It seems like everyone wants this perfect, voilà!, peaches-and-cream relationship. We can't tell you how many times people reach out to us looking for a cheat code. Sorry to tell you, but we don't have one. No matter who you meet—it doesn't matter how sexy, financially strong or weak, how spiritual they are—you're going to have to practice and put in the work. So, you might as well go on and get those romantic movies out of your head! Relationships are hard. Also, many people come into a new relationship and think their past has nothing to do with it. Some of us need to heal our trauma. And every relationship comes with new tests. Use what you've already been through as your textbook so that you don't overlook negative signs or repeat negative habits yourself. Think back on the lessons you learned then and apply them.

Here are a few exercises that we think can help bring you closer to each other:

- Go on a cheap date for under $20 just like you used to when you were kids or had less money. Come together to agree upon what it will be and what you will do together to make it as fun as possible for as little money as possible. Take the worldly expectations out of your relationship and invite the spirit of simplicity.

- Schedule a date night where you interview your partner about how you can best serve them and make them feel supported. Ask questions like, "What makes you feel safe? When do you feel happiest? What do you need from me that I could do better or am not doing at all right now? What do I do well that makes you feel supported?" Be sure to use "I" statements, where you affirmatively say what you need rather than focusing on what you think or believe the other person doesn't do. For example, DO say: "I feel supported when…"; "I love it when…"; "I feel happiest when you do…"; rather than "You never…"; "You don't…"; and the like. Then switch!

- Identify an area where you'd like to come into agreement with your partner. Listen to their perspective on the issue as though you were sitting in their shoes. Look for ways they make sense, have a good point, and are right. Let them know when you agree with them or like what they say. Then share your point of view with your partner, looking at the issue through your vantage point. The idea here isn't to win, or be right, or to just wait 'til they stop talking so you can make your point. Instead of looking for what's wrong, keep your spirit open to what's most important—and that is the connectivity and unity found in agreement. Then make a list of all the places you agree. Agree that you agree in these areas, then move forward with those things in common. Now watch God work!

CHAPTER 3

SUBMISSION 101
The Head vs. the Neck

FANTASIA

After we learned to take off our crowns, we began practicing submission. It's funny, but we never talked about it until after the whole situation with the *Breakfast Club* interview. It was just something we naturally began to do. But submission wasn't difficult once we'd stopped fighting each other and our inner demons and began to align ourselves under God.

KENDALL

Submission is very controversial to many people. People teach a lot of different things about it, and sometimes men teach it from a place of suppression and use Scripture to serve their selfish perspectives. We're not about that. The way we see it, submission is a biblical concept God has provided to help organize a spiritually based marriage and family. It is not something that a partner does alone; it's a balancing act between a husband and a wife.

The Bible tells women to submit to their husbands and tells men to love their wives as Christ loved and led the church (see Eph. 5:21–33). Christ is indeed King, but most of the time men like to overlook the fact that Christ led by serving. Everything Christ did was about helping another individual. He washed His disciples' feet and gave alms of forgiveness and repentance. He didn't throw His crown around, or wield His power, or perform miracles to show off or stroke His ego. In fact, the only time He asked anything for Himself was in the Garden of Gethsemane, when He didn't want to endure crucifixion. But even then, He surrendered and said, "Yet not my will, but yours be done" (Luke 22:42), once again surrendering to God's will above His own power and capabilities.

So God is basically telling couples, "Serve each other," and in serving others your true power will be realized. Serve her vision; serve his needs; serve her emotions; serve his pride; serve the misunderstandings. It's not, "You're the woman; you cook, you clean, you surrender, you tolerate whatever I do, and you lie on your back when I want you to." It's the complete opposite. But many men have made it into those things so that they don't have to raise the bar of their character. They use religion to suppress when spirituality is supposed to set everybody free. Christ demonstrated the total opposite of anything involving enslavement, suppression, or oppression. Everything was about being set free, being able to have the veil torn so that we could go directly to God; again, not being subjected to the dependence of any other man as had been made custom and tradition.

I tend to think of things from a business perspective. I think of "submission" as being like the name on a building, a title of sorts. But all the operations, mechanisms, and logistics inside involve people serving one another, and that gives the name on the outside the power that it is known for. In our home, I lead my wife by serving her dreams, by serving her emotions, by understanding the way she communicates. I will get up and bust down the kitchen if it's dirty. It's not about me being a dominant force.

FANTASIA

I think most women would run from a man who's trying to teach them submission. Come to think of it, it shouldn't be taught more than it is demonstrated. It's in your walk; it's in your talk. Like Christ. You just walk the way you need to walk, and I'm gonna walk the way I need to walk. I'm gonna do what I do for you, and you do what you do for me. Ken and I don't even talk about it. Sorry to disappoint you, but we don't have monthly "submission meetings"!

Part of the reason it was so easy for me to line up with him is that, as a vocalist and performer, I have been practicing submission for most of my life.

I'm a soul singer, but my voice is a gift from God and it's for God. Starting when I was just a girl, people would get saved in church because of my voice, and I have been using it to make people happy ever since. My mother has an amazing singing voice, and musically my father is a genius—just out of this world. From the time I was little they performed together. When I turned five, my dad started to teach me how to sing.

"How do you want me to sing it?" I'd ask. Then he would sing, and I would imitate the notes and words. When I couldn't follow his vocals, he would use his hands to show me when to move my voice up and down. I would enjoy seeing him smile and be happy. We would practice for hours; it was no joke. Then he would bring in my brothers, Rico and Teeny, and we would sing our parts together. In our group, the Barrino Family, my dad directed us and played the bass; my mother, who has a powerhouse voice, wrote and sang most of the songs. Rico would also sing tenor, Teeny was the alto, and I was the soprano. We each had our role; we each had to blend with the others. The purpose of our music was to give our gifts back to God and to glorify Him.

Even though you know me as a solo artist, when our family sang, I was almost never out front. I had maybe three songs out of all our music. In our group, whoever wasn't singing the solo would have to figure out whose notes were missing. Like, when Rico was singing, Teeny would take his notes. We would figure out whose voice fits where; who's gonna lead next week; who's gonna fall back.

But I never wanted just to stay in the church. I dreamed of singing in stadiums and on the award shows. Fast-forward to *Idol*. Each week, my job was to select songs that made people happy. Now I was singing in front of the whole wide world. So I needed to pick songs not just because I liked them, but because the older folks who would actually dial the phone would vote for them, and because young folks who may not know the songs might like them after the songs had been introduced to them. That's why I sang every genre of music. Everybody loves Stevie Wonder, Bonnie Raitt, and Elvis, so I sang their songs, songs the public would love.

On *Idol*, I also had to consider the other contestants. For example, I couldn't hog all the interview time. I would think, *Okay, 'Tasia, think what you're gonna say, how much time you're going to take to say it, and how you're going to say it, so it doesn't offend the other performers, then move out.*

All these experiences involved submitting to something greater than myself—submitting my gift to God, submitting to my father as he trained me, submitting to my role in our family group, submitting to the process in hopes that I would win. Along the way, I learned how powerful it is for people to submit a part of themselves to come together to do something greater than themselves.

The Starting Lineup

KENDALL

There continues to be a certain level of confusion about—and therefore, a feeling of rejection toward—the idea of submission in a marriage. A grave misunderstanding of the original text in its entirety has led to a rejection of the scriptural blueprint that the apostle Paul provided for a righteous marriage. Many people talking about submission quote Ephesians 5:22 and stop there: "Wives, submit yourselves to your own husbands, as you do to the Lord." But when you study the text in Ephesians 5—from verse 22 through verse 29—it leaves no room for misinterpretation that both the husband and the wife are to submit to one another in godly harmony:

Wives, submit yourselves to your own husbands as you do to the Lord. For the husband is the head of the wife as Christ is the head of the church, his body, of which he is the Savior. Now as the church submits to Christ, so also wives should submit to their husbands in everything.

Husbands, love your wives, just as Christ loved the church and gave himself up for her to make her holy, cleansing her by the washing with water through the word, and to present her to himself as a radiant church, without stain or wrinkle or any other blemish, but holy and blameless. In this same way, husbands ought to love their wives as their own bodies. He who loves his wife loves himself. After all, no one ever hated their own body, but they feed and care for their body, just as Christ does the church.

To be honest, I could drop the mic right here because 90 percent of the mishandling of the word "submission" has been based simply on people believing that the heavenly command rests solely on the woman. Nothing could be further from the truth.

Yes, in a marriage based on the original design that God created, it is the man who is established as the head of the marriage. The head seated spiritually is just like that of the head positioned physically on the body, where it is less about rulership and much more about responsibility. The wife is commissioned with submitting to her husband's headship with her strength, love, support, and loyalty. These are symbols of her own power and meekness—I define meekness as being power under self-control—because her contribution is a voluntary offering. Same as in our natural bodies concerning the head. If the body chooses paralysis and the body refuses to contribute, can the head force it to respond into action? No, there must be agreement between the body and the mind in order to produce forward motion. The husband's responsibility is to be a direct reflection of Christ's posture toward the church and to demonstrate similar love toward his wife. All throughout the gospel, Christ demonstrates and reiterates that though He is the Head over the church, He exercises His power by healing others, washing the feet of others, and dying for the sake of others, even when they rejected Him. Every angelic resource and form of divine power He possessed during the time the gospel was written was used toward the benefit of others, never for Himself. There were many occasions where Christ could have flexed His muscle and ego, such as when Satan tempted Him three times in the desert, or when He was ridiculed and beaten in the Roman courts, or when He was finally crucified for crimes He did not commit.

This is the example we as husbands are supposed to walk in. Are we using our power and strength to help heal our wives? Have we lost our willingness to humbly wash the feet of her emotional needs?

Are we willing to allow our pride and arrogance to be crucified in order that her purpose and destiny can manifest? If we are not operating in this manner, then we have not earned the rewards of our wives' trust in our leadership and direction. Our wives won't find the comfort and confidence to follow us into the unknown unless they smell the aroma of God's presence permeating our prayers and daily conduct.

When a man is walking in the highest power source on earth, which is humility, and his wife is submitting her power source of love and meekness, they will walk in unity and power.

FANTASIA

Though lots of women think about submission in a negative way, from my perspective as a woman, spiritual submission isn't about giving up control to a man. My husband is the head of our relationship, but I'm the neck. The head doesn't turn and look at anything without involving the neck.

The woman brings her own gifts, her own talents, her own abilities to the marriage or relationship. A husband who engages in spiritually centered leadership makes it very easy for his mate to line up with him and God, whether she's knowledgeable about submission or not.

He also lines up with her.

It's about mutually deciding to treat your partner as a king or a queen. As I said on *The Breakfast Club*, the queen is the most powerful piece on the chessboard. She can make more moves than any other piece.

KENDALL

The husband submits to his wife; she submits to her husband; and they both submit themselves to God. Christ voluntarily put

Himself in a position to go through every single violent, despicable, disgraceful act to express His love. Men are supposed to walk in Christ's demonstration, where we're leading by serving, guiding, and surrendering. But that's not what a lot of men do. For instance, how often do we as men allow our feet to be pierced so that we don't run, or leave situations, but instead stand firm in emotional strength? How often do we open our arms and allow our hands to be pierced by denying ourselves something we want, or relinquishing control in a situation to promote harmony? How often are we willing to put on that crown of thorns and pierce our own understanding and look at something from her point of view and not let what we think and feel dominate, so that something more beautiful can come forward?

First Corinthians 7:14 says the woman's righteousness will cover the husband's and the husband's righteousness will cover the wife's. And because both the husband and the wife surrender to God, when the natural world tries to pull you outside the lane of your vows, God protects you. The Most High will help you navigate through the quicksand of emotional confusion to get you back on solid ground.

But submission has to be earned. A woman has to see certain qualities, attributes, and leadership capabilities in her mate in order to feel like she can begin to even consider relinquishing certain duties and responsibilities, as well as sharing certain feelings and emotions. Ideally, the marriage will be Spirit-filled from the beginning, but people can develop both spiritually and submissively over time.

FANTASIA

My musical career is a testimony to the power that is possible after submission has been earned.

I've had the chance to work with some big-name producers and artists: Quincy Jones, Elton John, Ron Fair, and more. Whoever I am working with, the sounds I create have to work for their vision.

Once Clive Davis—the former president of Columbia Records and probably the most accomplished music producer in the country—invited me to sing the song "Put You Up on Game" with Aretha Franklin. I asked him to put me on the phone with her, so I could ask her how she wanted me to sing it. The last thing I wanted was to be with the Queen of Soul, and sing all over her song, and have her not like it.

When we got on the phone, she said, "Just do you."

"Okay," I told her. But I knew not to "go in" on a legend's record and try to outdo her! I fell back and submitted my voice and my gift to hers.

And check it: Being unwilling to submit to people who have earned it can cost you. I've had times when producers would want me to do a certain thing and I'd be like, "Okay, but I think Clive's gonna want it different; he's gonna make me come back." And sure enough, he did want something different, and we had to go back into the studio and do it again.

I'm not gonna name any names, but there was one person I worked with who I wouldn't submit my gift to. It was the worst experience I'd ever had in a studio. I've worked with some of the greatest and had never felt disrespected, but this person thought they could tell me what I could and could not do. I was like, "Hold up; wait a minute! You're putting me in an atmosphere I've never been in before. Nope! Uh-uh…This ain't it!" I had never left a recording session until then, but I walked out of several sessions with this artist.

There's just nothing like working with a producer you trust. You can submit your gift to them and know that they will take care of it. Sometimes I've had a producer tell me, "Fantasia, there's a feeling that I know you have in you." I may not ever have tapped into that part of myself before, but seeing their excitement and trusting them, I could say, "Okay, let's try!" Practicing submission to someone I know I'm safe with allows me to produce my best music.

What I was looking for when I was single, and what I've found in Kendall, is someone to get together with me to accomplish great things. There are many women who submit in their daily lives and may not have considered it until now. As women, we submit to our careers, to our children, to our church ministries, all the way down to our homeowners' associations. We do what is required when it is in our power to do so and, most times, we receive little to nothing in return. The takeaway here is that we are more than capable of offering submission in a marriage; it simply takes the right man and the right atmosphere for us to feel comfortable.

KENDALL

I'm glad you brought that up, Queen, because there are limits to the practice of submission.

There's no room for submission in an abusive relationship. That's not submission; that's control; that's suppression; that's aggression.

FANTASIA

Lord knows, I've been in too many relationships like that. I don't want that for any woman.

KENDALL

In many relationships the God component is nowhere to be found. No woman is biblically bound by those laws when they are not being upheld and reciprocated by the man.

And let's keep it 100: Many times, we men want to create our own power current that isn't connected to God. The problem with that is, we have no power source alone. When we operate on our own, we have nothing to plug into. So, you get only vanity, and the insecurity that produces control and domination. Women can feel when a man's not standing inside the will of God. They often feel triggered by the energy, so they rightly resist it.

FANTASIA

When Ken lines up correctly, not only does he not have to demand anything from me, he doesn't even have to ask.

KENDALL

She's comfortable when I'm operating in the will of God. But as soon as I step outside of it, disconnect, and start to operate within my own might, I behave forcefully. Anytime you attempt to force someone, you're operating at the lowest level of consciousness. My wife can feel it and she resists. Anytime you operate in force, that is not love, and where love is absent only fear exists. And no man can lead another person when he's operating from a place of fear.

FANTASIA

That's when King might find himself washing his own clothes and making his own meals.

KENDALL

When she's mad at me, Queen is the master of cooking a one-portion meal! I'll be sitting in another room smelling what I believe is a feast, only to walk into the kitchen and see no dishes, no prepared plates or containers in the fridge.

When a man steps outside of the righteousness of God and tries to create his own line of authority, his wife rightfully should not abide by that.

FEELING UNSAFE? GET HELP NOW

For various reasons, we both have found ourselves in violent and traumatic situations. We don't want you to experience the fear, harm, anxiety, or PTSD that comes when you've been mistreated in any way or stalked. If you fear for your safety in your relationship or are experiencing emotional, verbal, mental, or physical abuse, help is available, whether you're a woman or a man.

The National Domestic Violence Hotline can help you understand the warning signs of abuse, create a safety plan for you and your kids, identify local resources, get legal help, protect your pets, and more. It's free, confidential, and open 24-7. Contact https://www.thehotline.org or 800-799-SAFE (7233).

Fall Back to Spring Forward

KENDALL

Compromise is essential to every relationship, but in many areas of our society, the spirit of compromise is being smothered. You used to see couples at church who had been married for sixty years. Can you imagine how much compromise had to take place during that time?

FANTASIA

But we're becoming a selfish generation: You hear, "I'm a [this]; I'm a [that]." Even lots of the music is all about fame, popularity, social media: "Look at me, look at me!"

Selfishness smothers the spirit of compromise, where you're supposed to behave selflessly. When we behave selfishly, we leave no room for collaboration; no room for cohabitation; no room for cooperation. We're just buying time until the issue comes to a head.

The most successful musicians know that everything shouldn't be about you.

For example, when a writer or a producer calls or invites me to appear in the lineup for their show, there is a reason why they want me to sing each of the songs they give me. Sometimes it's because they have a story to tell—something they went through, or a part of their journey. Maybe they have the gift to be able to write it, but when they speak it, it doesn't emotionally move a roomful of people. That's where the gift of my voice and the ability to tell a story musically come in.

They write the words, then I learn the story and find out why they want me to sing it. Usually there is an emotion they're looking for in the song and they think I can express it. Or maybe there's something about my tone, or they believe that I have the ability to put the right emotion in the right place.

Then, after they tell me their story, I take their words and I can almost visualize the scenes. I'm like, "Oh, that's a joyful word; that has to be a painful word; this has to be an up; that has to be a down." Then I use my voice to express their story. Is it a love song? I'll sing the sweet notes and tones that feel like love. Is it about healing a broken heart? I'll sing some sounds of encouragement. Does the audience need to be lifted up and feel empowered? I can sing those sounds too. They bring the words to the table and I provide the melody. My gift has to submit to and blend with their gift. By coming together, we create music and move people in a way that is greater than either of us could have created alone.

The same thing happens when I'm onstage. Musically and performance-wise, I practice submission. When there are several people sharing the stage, every performer has to wait their turn. You deliver your part, and then you fall back while the background singers do their thing. When it's time for the saxophone player to play a melody, you stand aside and allow the sax to inspire you. Once it's time for you to sing again, you sing in a manner where you blend with the other musicians. That's also what happens when you attend a musical or Broadway play—you're witnessing the performers and musicians submitting to somebody else's vision. At the same time, they're bringing their gifts and hoping to create something even better and more beautiful than the producers could ever imagine. Artistically, maybe next week as a singer your job will be to sing in the choir. In a choir, you submit your voice to blend with every voice in your section. A director can tell when somebody's too loud or off-key. They'll stop the song and say, "Somebody over there is pitchy," and expect you to correct yourself—to submit to the larger vision. In my imagination, this is also how it happens with God and the way He conducts the harmonies that He's looking for out of marriages.

As an artist, to get the most out of your gift, it's best not to have a selfish bone in your body. You hear a lot of stories about divas causing drama, but some of the most amazing performers can be very selfless. You have to give, do your part, then back up or move over to make room for the next person. I've been doing this for so long that there are times when I think I'd like to have a little bit of rudeness, a little bit of arrogance, but that's just not who I am.

You may have heard me sing "I'm His Only Woman" with Jennifer Hudson or seen the performance on YouTube. I have also performed onstage with her. Jennifer is a powerhouse! Real talk. She belts out most of her stuff. I can belt, too, but both of us belting doesn't produce the best performance if we do it at the same time. Artistically, I'm not going to try to out-belt and sing over her to prove my voice is powerful. I'm going to look for the pockets between where she is belting so that my singing complements hers. She will sing a major note and I will sing a minor note. Many times, when producers put two singers onstage together, they don't pick two vocal powerhouses. They'll pair a powerhouse with someone who has a totally different sound, or a vocal stylist, so they each have their own pocket. Their voices blend and they create something more beautiful than either would have created individually.

So, every time you listen to an amazing song, remember that you're listening to a lot of other people submitting—from the soloists, to the background singers, to the musicians.

Musically, surrender and compromise go together. I think marriage works the same way.

By the time you see me standing in front of an audience, I've not only learned my part, but I've also participated in the rehearsals, watched them on video, listened to my vocals, fixed the wrong notes, learned my steps, practiced the routine, been corrected, and fixed my errors. Afterward, I may watch and listen to recordings of the performance all night. The band, the cast, and I keep working on our performances in the same way that professional athletes do. There's always something that we could have done better. My feet may have blisters and calluses on them. I'm only in my mid-thirties and I already have bad knees. We put in an unbelievable amount of work so that our performance looks easy.

So now, if I go into the studio or onstage and do all these things to make other people happy, why wouldn't I bring that level of effort to my marriage? I want to bring joy to my fans, and I want to bring joy to my marriage. I want to see Ken smile; I want to see him happy;

I want to see him dancing in the kitchen and cracking jokes, just acting funny with me. I want my metaphorical voice to work together with his to create a great harmony, so I'm not singing over him and he's not singing over me. We each find our own pocket and sing a perfect ballad that inspires the people who hear it to want to try harder in their relationship or marriage.

KENDALL

Some men tend to get frustrated because their women aren't submitting the way they desire. But didn't Christ give His life knowing the church wasn't going to be loyal, wasn't going to be dedicated? That it would be inconsistent, and unfaithful? But He still gave Himself for His church, and we must do the same for our own wives who are our church. So even if your wife's not submitting the way you want her to submit—you're not getting your dinner cooked at six, you're not getting sex except on your birthday—as a man of God you still must give yourself for your wife. Too often we forget that no one forced us into this. We volunteered for marriage. We chose and agreed to uphold the vows and the unforeseen variables that are attached to all marriages. Many times, people read Scripture until it appears to confirm whatever they carry in their hearts, but then they don't go any further or read any more deeply to gain understanding of the message in full. This is especially true about men and submission.

Christ gave Himself to the church, but He gave Himself to a church that talked back, was stiff-necked, rebellious, inconsistent, idolatrous, and backsliding; and that church ultimately killed him. So a man whose wife doesn't submit to him still has to submit to Christ and give the best he has to offer her and wait for God to manifest His perfect will in the situation. Consider this—perhaps your wife is operating in a certain manner so that God can prune, refashion, and perfect something inside of you for His glory. Perhaps God is withholding the thing you are seeking from her in hopes that you would turn and seek it from Him instead. It's time we as men begin to seek the deeper mysteries of God that can be found only beneath the surface of our fleshly ambitions.

But I know that if I had said that to a group of men, it would be a quiet room.

FANTASIA

Early in our relationship, back when I was still a firecracker, there were several times when my blood was boiling, and I was mouthing off. Ken grabbed me, looked me in the eyes, and talked to me in a way no one had ever talked to me before. He was firm and gentle at the same time. Uncompromising in his principles but also very receptive to my emotions and perspective.

KENDALL

I told her, "I'm here now. You no longer have to carry that chip on your shoulder and that weight of protecting yourself from harm. Pass it over to me and let me take care of it."

FANTASIA

In that moment the whole world went away, the room went still; it was just me and him. I was like, "Hold up, maybe I shouldn't do that and maybe I shouldn't say that." I don't even care about the word "submission." A man had come into my life who was walking in a certain way that made me want to follow his example, but in the way a woman would do it. I had never experienced that before. My blood went from boiling to being just calmed right down.

KENDALL

In truth and in deed, the responsibility is on the man to set the tone. No matter what she does, no matter how she demonstrates, you still have to give the best of yourself.

FANTASIA

How he handled me and the things he said to me called me up to a higher level. The way he carried himself made me want to be a better woman. So, I was like, "You can calm me down and show me a different view?! Whatever path you're going on, I'm gonna take it. I'm following you!"

Everybody wants to get caught up on this word "submission." I just wanted to follow Ken's leadership because he had an usual peace and a calm spirit that I hungered for in my life. You can call that whatever you want. I'm gonna follow his path because I like what he's doing, and he showed me something new. From cooking, to parenting, to lovemaking, to business, to whatever else, he has shown me how to see everything in ways that are different from anything I had experienced before. When the kids start wilin' out, I call him first. He's calm. I like his methods; I've seen them work. Sometimes we do good cop, bad cop. So call it whatever you want; I call it, "I've found a partner; I like his style and we're gonna rock out." Just find you a partner, and if they have good methods and can get you to that finish line of victory, say, "Yes, I'm with you." But if your partner can't guide you safely, and you're both making dumb decisions from a spirit of disagreement, and you're digging deeper holes using selfish shovels, well, I can't tell you exactly what you should do but I think you already know the answer to that.

THE TAYLORS

Christ says, "Come follow Me and let the dead bury the dead," figuratively (see Matt. 8:22). In other words, "Let the people who want chaos, violence, drama, or whatever—let them have that and keep it among themselves. Come this way and let that be what it's going to be."

We've learned that in a marriage, submission requires mutual trust and for a man and a woman to share the same vision about where they're going. When God sees two people humbling themselves every day, taking the ego and self-idolatry out of the equation—because God will never be in the midst of any of that—and serving each other, He'll come in and turn around every misunderstanding, every disagreement, every unconstructive way you think and move you in the same direction on life's journey as one. Life can turn into a long and frustrating road trip when everybody wants to go their own way.

Now that you understand some of our beliefs and experiences with submission, we would like you to consider how submission might help you. Here are some questions to journal, think about, and discuss with each other:

- What concerns, if any, do you have about practicing submission? How could it help you? What areas do you see that could be problematic?
- Outside of your marriage, are there areas of life where you already practice submission? If so, what are those areas and who has earned your submission? What have been the good points and bad points?
- What gifts do you bring to your marriage that could be part of practicing submission?

- What are the areas in your relationship where you could naturally step forward or where it makes sense for you to fall back?
- In what areas in your life can you take one step closer to practicing submission?

CHAPTER 4

MISSING FOOTPRINTS

Being What You Have Not Seen

KENDALL

I was thirteen years old the only time I saw my father, and he was dying from leukemia. My mom asked me if I wanted to go meet him. I was like, "Yeah, of course." So my first time on a plane was going to Mississippi to meet him. It was one of the most exciting—and disappointing—experiences of my life. You're excited 'cause you get to see your father, but at the same time, now he's dying; there's no hero in him. He was walking around, skinny as a stick, tubes in his veins and pulling an IV pole. The one thing I remember most is that he didn't do much talking to me. He spent more time talking to my mom; he didn't connect with me a lot during that visit.

The next time I had a chance to see my father was eighteen months later, when my mom got the call that he had passed away. She asked me if I wanted to go to the funeral. I was like, "No, I don't know him." Even as an adult, I don't regret not going. What I regret is not connecting with my other family members on his side. I let my anger toward him cause me to be disconnected from getting to know my family.

So I didn't have a lot of good examples to show my own son when I became a teenage father just two years later. But I was determined to be in his life even though my father hadn't been in mine. When I got out of jail, I wanted to build the bond that my years in the streets had taken away. Nothing on earth mattered to me more than making my son proud of me and finding a level of success that could not be taken away from me.

But by the time I came home, I had lost everything. I had to start over. I was living with my mama, working for $7.25 an hour, loading things in a warehouse, taking out trash, cleaning, sweeping floors. I used to borrow my mom's car to pick up my son. I used to ask my mother for money to feed him while he was with me. It was humbling.

When I started my trucking company eighteen months later, I was still sleeping on my mother's floor. My son slept on the floor with me. He saw me on my back; he watched me get on all fours; then on my knees; and then he watched me stand up as a man, and that taught him something. It was involuntary on my end because it was not the best situation; I did not choose it. But it taught him a lot and he has so much respect for me having seen that level of transparency most men withold from their sons' view.

The Seed Rises Up

FANTASIA

Many of us have big dreams as far as relationships, but we've grown up in families or communities where we haven't had role models to help guide us to relationship success. Good or bad, experiences you have during your early years can rub off on you and affect how you see your life in the long term, including your adult relationships. Some of us have been exposed to generational curses, where bad habits and addictions that started before we were born somehow get passed down to us. Those of us who haven't had good role models often look to examples on social media, which have their own sets of problems, including the ability to convince us to strive for an image of ourselves that isn't even close to the description God wrote next to our names. But we have the power to break those cycles so that we can create relationships that work for us. To do that, it's important to let our true selves show and to follow God's path and the wisdom of people we trust.

KENDALL

Both my wife and I are overcoming generational curses and believe that facing them can help any relationship become and remain healthier. Bibically speaking, a generational curse is physical, spiritual, mental, or emotional sinful behavior passed on from generation to generation. These tendencies and behaviors get passed through the family as a consequence of people's actions, not because God has cursed you and you can't escape them.[1] They are harmful by-products of the unrighteous decisions made by others who came before you.

---

1. Hank Hanegraaff, "Are Generational Curses Biblical?," June 19, 2020, Christianity.com, https://www.christianity.com/wiki/christian-life/are-generational-curses-biblical.html.

Some generational curses that come to mind are curses of broken marriages, traditions of infidelity, repeated cycles of teenage pregnancies, and deep-rooted drug and alcohol abuse, just to name a few. I never knew my father. Turns out he never had a tight relationship with his father. When you are a child, you do not know why your father, or perhaps your mother, is not there. You may want to excuse them, but at some point, that cycle has to be addressed.

Because the behaviors that contributed to the generational curse happened before we came on the scene, we may not know another way of existence. Sometimes, the generational curses are invisible and we just assume they're normal. When you are used to dysfunction, and you are used to chaos, and you are used to pain and trauma and rejection and darkness, when everybody around you is in it, you do not realize that there's even another option until you get around another family, or play sports, or go over to your coach's house and you're like, "This is different. You actually like each other. You all get along. You all actually sit at the table. You all hug each other. You all say, 'I love you.'"

So, sometimes you can be unaware that you are battling a generational curse and you are taking that to school; you are taking it to your job. You are taking it from relationship to relationship because that dysfunction has become a part of your makeup and it is a part of your identity. That's why generational curses can lie hidden and dormant. But when you are exposed to other people and ways of living, you suddenly have something to compare it to. If your whole family rocks a certain way and moves a certain way, you do not know that this is not right or the correct approach to living. It is your norm until either you are confronted with some new information or you gain exposure outside of your environment. You may have to intentionally enter into or even create a different atmosphere so you can see something different.

Because generational curses are not of this world, the prescription or the cure is not of this world either. Simply put, we have to progress past the point of trying to diagnose and remedy supernatural ailments with natural prescriptions. Doing that, in a sense, is a way human beings try to maintain a sense of control and ownership over real estate that belongs to God. There isn't going to be a pill, a tonic, or an over-the-counter means of bringing healing to spiritual diseases. The only cure is to combat them by exposing ourselves to a righteous posture of living.

In my case, breaking my main generational curse was a matter of making sure that I was present in Trey's life. That was the cure. I'd started working on this decades before Queen and I got married, and it was challenging. I could feel that curse on me at times. There were times when I just could not move forward with it, or I got frustrated, or I clocked out of dealing with it. But that definitely was a curse that I had to address and overcome in my life for myself, for my son, and for my grandsons.

My greatest accomplishment is seeing my son stand as a good father, and also by his not having his first son until he was in his twenties. I am also proud of being able to create generational wealth even though we never had a millionaire in our family lineage. Being able to break through those barriers and inspire my little brother and my son to aspire to more is something I consider part of my legacy.

FANTASIA

Baby, I'm so proud of you!

It is good to know those things and acknowledge our successes. But some people are like, "I do not believe in generational curses; everybody is just who they are." No, I believe that when the seed of that tree is planted and rises up, certain things from your great-grandmother, grandmother, and your mother pass through.

I am breaking through generational curses too. For me, there's a double whammy because I have curses on my mother's side and on my father's side. I already told you about how I have to watch my drinking and my mouth. On my mother's side, they have always been very open with sitting me down and letting me know about two generational curses in particular. For one, my grandmother did not graduate from high school, my mother did not graduate, and I did not graduate until I went back and got my GED as an adult. There's also the fact that my grandmother had her first child at seventeen; my mother had my older brother at seventeen; I had Zion at seventeen; and one of my cousins had her first baby at seventeen. I mean, at some point you've got to start looking at certain things and try to understand what's going on instead of taking the easy way out and ruling everything as a coincidence. Calling patterns like that coincidences removes a sense of responsibility, and it's that very thing that is needed to reverse and break certain cycles in your bloodline. My grandma did not sit me down and say, "Hey, 'Tasia, it's time to go have a baby. I was seventeen, so you have one when you are seventeen." And nobody said, "I want to talk to you about something that happened when I was your age so you will be better off." All these things were happening and lining up, but nobody had that conversation with me until after. I was like, "Dang, I did not even know, Mom"; "I did not even know, Grandma."

Fortunately, we all came out with dope testimonies. And either way, children are gifts from God and, if God gave you that child, you have to figure it out because parenting doesn't come with a parenting book. But my experience was so much like my grandmother's, and so much like my mother's and my aunt's that I had to take the initiative and sit Zion down and reveal to her the pattern that was snowballing through the women in our family. I believe that there are generational things that you have to cut from your life. These kinds of patterns have roots.

I have talked to Zion about the history of women in my family. I'm proud that she is doing her part to break the curse and go for her own goals and dreams. I told her, "Zion, children are a gift from God, but I want you to wait and make sure you get your education." And it makes me proud to see my daughter approaching her twentieth birthday with no children at this time.

The same is true as far as just finding bad relationships. My grandmother's father stepped out on his family. She was a side child, so she did not get the love that she felt she deserved. Even though her sisters and her brothers brought her in and loved her, she still had that hole in her heart. My grandmother's first husband was an alcoholic. So, he spent most of his time drinking and he would call them names. They grew up with that. When that type of environment becomes the norm, it is doomed to repeat itself. I have also experienced abuse in relationships, starting when I was a teenager.

I already shared that on my father's side, I come from a family where everybody is musically talented and a performer. We could connect through our music, and musically, we could all get along. We would all sing together and be happy. That was a wonderful blessing! But in our talented, performing family, everyone wanted to please and make everybody in the audience happy, and be the life of the party. I kind of took on a role like, "Let us just make everybody happy and please everybody." But anxiety came with that. There were so many musical geniuses in one room, sometimes I would think, *This person knows it better* or *That person could do it better. Am I really that talented?* And since I was trained as an entertainer, I was always thinking, *I gotta please people. I got to say yes to these people. I got to make them happy. I have to get onstage. I gotta kill it.*

My family was so talented but there weren't enough opportunities for all of them, so I feel there was a lot of competition. It seemed like everybody ended up fighting with each other. For some reason, we were never able to experience the love we expressed sonically within our relationships with one another. We couldn't figure out how to match our love of music with our love of family. Eventually, we ended up with a family that does not speak as much as I'd like. I guess you can say that the music stopped playing at some point.

My extended family may have struggled, but in my own family, I want both love and good relationships to exist—and I'll fight for that.

KENDALL

In addition to breaking the cycle of fatherlessness, I also know that alcoholism and drug abuse exist in my family. I am an '80s baby, so a lot of people around me were affected by crack, and I saw it. I remember those things; my life was impacted by it. So I am very aware of that addiction in my bloodline just waiting to cripple me and burden me with all the things that come with it. During my younger years, and even when I was running the streets, if I had a couple of drinks I was backing out. You are not going to catch me out there making a fool of myself. So, I have practiced a great sense of self-control and discipline to combat that in my own personal life. I know this isn't true for everyone, but for me that has been the cure.

As we blend our family, we're trying to be what we have not seen. We don't have an internal playbook we can follow. I constantly read books about leadership, relationships, and communication to help me fill the void left by a missing father and a lack of suitable mentorship. I'm learning to rock off of my intuition and gut feelings while wrestling with the wrong definitions of "manhood" that our society pushes in the face of men every single day.

FANTASIA

For me and Ken, we didn't really hear a lot of melodic notes and harmony in the marriages we saw when we were growing up. We didn't see or hear it, but when we were in the presence of a good marriage, we knew it. Something about the way they loved, the touchy-touchy-feely part of it. Like, you ever notice around Christmastime, you put on a Christmas album and it just changes the whole atmosphere in the house? My grandmother used to play the Temptations' Christmas album or the Mariah Carey album and I would be so happy. The music would just put me in a good mood, especially "Silent Night" by the Temptations. I would be like, "Whatever you want, Grandma!" That's the kind of love and warmth that Kendall and I want to flow through our household. That Luther, Aretha, Whitney Houston, and Anita Baker kind of love I listened to growing up. We want that kind of energy to flow through us, so we can instill it in our kids and our home can be touchy-feely and our children can be in a great mood. I want that for my family and I will fight for it.

So when I speak to the younger people I know, or when I speak to certain nieces and nephews, I want to let them know. "Hey, that is a generational thing. You have got to break it," I tell them. "Auntie's been breaking off the curses in her life, so you got to start breaking these things off in your life in order to have a healthy relationship, in order to be the best mother, the best friend, sister, and so on, in order to have a business or a life of success found in the simple things. These are things you got to break off in your life."

You may already know that I'm a big fan of affirmations. During a very dark point in my life I started posting affirmations on a mirror each day. "You are strong," I wrote. "You are wise." I wrote phrases like these on Post-it Notes and they've helped me ever since. Affirmations are short positive statements that help you speak life into your own spirit and challenge you to overcome thoughts that are negative and can sabotage you. I had to overcome things I'd say to myself when I was younger—my beliefs that I was ugly, that I was skinny, that my lips were too big.

Writing and then speaking affirmations is a powerful tool for breaking generational curses. First, ask a parent or one of your loved ones what unhelpful patterns they have seen passing through the generations in your family, because at times it can be a challenge to recognize our own weaknesses. Then find a quiet space away from your partner and kids where you can be by yourself—it can be someplace in nature like a park, or your bedroom, the bathroom, or even a closet or the laundry room. Make a list of the negative patterns, then for each one write three positive affirmations. State them affirmatively, in a positive way. Let's just say you have a bad relationship with your mom. Instead of, "Please help me stop being so impatient with my mother," say, "I notice all the good things about my mom," or "I think positively when I speak to and about my mother," or "My mother is always there for me"—whatever is appropriate.

Copy your affirmations onto Post-it Notes, then stick them around your house—on the bathroom mirror, the kitchen cabinet, by the front door, where you put your keys, on your makeup counter, on the refrigerator, on the kitchen cabinets. Every time you see an affirmation, repeat it out loud. Also, look at yourself in the mirror every day and speak words like, "I allow the spirit of peace into my life. I invite a spirit of cooperation into my day. I am genuinely happy for my sister's success." Once you start to recognize the generational patterns for yourself, you can know what to pray for and how to speak positively into the future you want to see. This will allow you to switch up your posture and reshape the way that you view yourself and your life.

It's Hard to Be What You Have Not Seen

FANTASIA

It's also important to have role models who can help provide healthy examples of the type of relationship you want to create.

As far as providers, my mother and father were real role models for me. They were go-getters; they made sure that we had a roof over our heads, even though High Point isn't a rich city and we didn't have a lot. My mom was a real good example of womanhood as well. I remember all the times she would turn the stove on when we did not have heat. When we had no lights, she would light the candles. Sometimes, we did not have a lot of groceries, but we were always able to eat. We had grits every night—we had grits with bacon, bologna, and eggs. We ate every day. She is a real role model for me.

I remember one time when we did not have any food, and it was snowing outside.

My mom—if it is snowing outside, that means there is some black ice somewhere and she is NOT driving. Well, at one point, we got a lot of snow and so my mom put on two pairs of pants, a bunch of socks, threw about three or four coats on, and headed out to get us food.

"I do not want you to go out in the snow," I said as I stood at the door crying.

"All of you, stay here," she told my brother. Then my mother walked fifteen minutes to the grocery store, and she came walking back with the groceries in her hands.

My father was out on the road a lot as a long-distance truck driver, always trying to make ends meet. But even though he wasn't always in town, his presence was always in our home. Most of the kids who lived around us didn't have daddies. They had left, were in jail, or were dead. But my father stayed and I loved him for that. I will never forget the sound of his boots walking down the hall in the morning. His presence in our home made me feel loved and secure.

KENDALL

Shout-out to my mom, as well. When Hurricane Hugo came through, it turned Gastonia upside down. I remember we were driving somewhere up on Union Road, and we could not get farther down, so she tied some plastic bags around our feet, and we walked through it together.

Another time, the toilet fell through the bottom floor and to the basement. We had one furnace that we had to light with a match, and my brother, Robert, would always try to sit in front of it with his covers and block it for himself. But you know, she made it work, alone and without the support of a man, raising two boys.

My mom would work throughout the week, and on the weekends, we went to the flea market, and she would sell little figurines, L'Arôme, or Avon, or just sell something—it could be brownies. My mom would sell something and make her hustle. Looking back, it was truly unfair for my mother to have to endure those hardships alone. My younger brother and I have separate fathers and they were both absent during our toughest times. Not only am I determined to always be a presence and provider for my children, but I will also be a support system and a rock that my Queen will always be able to depend on. That is the cure.

FANTASIA

I also learned a lot about the type of woman I wanted to be by watching other women around me. In High Point, North Carolina, there were two different types of women that I would see. One type, represented by my grandmother and my mother, was a woman who was meek, mild; she loved God, she loved her family. The other kind were rah-rah-rah women who weren't respectful, would embarrass their husbands, fight with their families, and do reckless stuff. I'm sure there were other models of womanhood, but I focused on those two, and even though I was a firecracker, there was always something inside me that wanted to be more like my grandmother and my mother.

But I didn't always see great examples of a marriage. By the time I was a teenager, things with my parents had gotten rough. It's hard having a large family when things are tight, and I am sure that played a role in adding stress to their marriage. Trust was broken in certain areas, which caused the romance and spark to slowly fade away. On my mother's side, my grandmother took a lot of stuff from my mother's father. My grandfather was an alcoholic and there are many hurtful experiences that come from battling with that disease. From the stories that my mother tells me, when he was good, he was good, but when he was bad, he was bad. Most of the time when he was bad, he was drinking.

I was blessed that I had my mom's guidance and my grandmother's example. My mother cooked every day and there was food on the table for my father; our clothes were clean. My mom was a fighter for relationships. My grandmother went through a lot, but her character never changed. She was a sweet woman, and a loving woman, and a woman of the community and helping everybody. I saw good guidelines.

So I look to these women as an example to say, "Okay, I can go through a lot of the situations that Ken and I have gone through and still make it through. I can also go through situations that would make most women say, 'I'm out.'" I come from a tough line of women. I was taught to fight for love; to make it work; to pray over it; to keep a strong relationship with God. I brought a lot of that with me from my home and I think it helps in our marriage.

KENDALL

Though my wife had strong women as role models, we share so many things in common as it relates to this marriage. We're trying to take our relationship to another level and be something that we have not seen. And it's easy to say that you're just not gonna be what you saw that you didn't like. It's easy to say, "Okay, well, we're just not gonna be that." But the hard thing is to define for yourself, "Okay, then, what and who are we gonna be?"

My main mission is to be a God-fearing man, a gentleman, a successful man, who can walk with integrity under any circumstance. Men need something to model themselves after so they can be the men that God called them to be. Because I believe when men stand up, the women have something they can trust, and then the communities and the world will follow suit. But until men get in position, there's no way we can expect the world to improve. I don't care what laws get changed, what organizations sprout up and catch fire, what policies get rewritten, until men decide to be uncompromising in their integrity, and their honor toward God, and their standards of character, I don't think that this world will improve from how it's looking right now. And there is no neutral zone in nature, so something is either improving or sadly declining.

As far as what a good father looks like, I haven't seen it. As far as what a good husband looks like, I haven't seen that either. By that I mean that I don't take how marriages appear to be on face value because life is filled with smoke and mirrors. Knowing the struggles that I have had to overcome in my own marriage, I never assume that Billy Bob and Susie Mae down the street truly are what they present themselves to be. I've never had deep-level conversations with a man who has a solid marriage, who can show me a blueprint or be transparent and share advice of how he's dealt with conflict, how he's dealt with emotional friction, or how he's dealt with raising children that are not biologically his, or how to communicate—these are things that I'm learning as I go.

And it's not enough for me to see a pastor and be like, "Okay, yeah, he's got it down pat. Because that's no different than looking at men on Instagram and assuming they're doing the right thing. You don't know the dynamics that are taking place beyond that picture any more than you know the dynamics that go on beyond the pulpit."

Letting the Spirit Lead

KENDALL

Since I'm in the game without a playbook that I can follow, I discipline myself to follow God's lead by studying the Scriptures. I also read articles and different books on leadership, relationships, and communication to try to get information from third parties, so I can look at mistakes other men have made and solutions that have worked for others that I never would have considered on my own. At the same time, I'm trying to be an example of how to interact with a woman now that my stepson Dallas is seeing life through his own eyes. I try to help Trey prepare himself to be a husband and to function at a greater level of manhood and leadership as he begins to experience the demands that come with success.

Some days I knock it out of the park and some days I fail, but I try to be fair to myself because I hold myself to a scriptural standard in what some would call an unrighteous world. It's one thing if you know the right thing to do and you intentionally choose not to do it. It's another thing to fail in certain situations because you don't have any foundational teachings and examples to fall back on to reinforce some of your decisions, behaviors, and actions.

I'm really trying to let the Spirit lead me; I'm trying to rock off my intuition and my gut feeling. A lot of it is trial by combat. A lot of it is blowing something up in the moment, then realizing, *Okay, that didn't work*, then trying something else. A lot of it is looking at the ashes of my mistake and saying, "Yeah, that definitely ain't the way to do it." I'm trying my best just not to keep circling around the same mountain of mistakes; rather, I'm trying to take the fall and extract a lesson that I can build on as I courageously climb again.

So, though men are following me, I can't always tell them all the right things to do. Sometimes I am able to say, "Listen, brother, this works." But I also share my mistakes, because those are even more valuable. I can say, "I made the same mistake; I just got out the doghouse; that don't work; don't do that; find another way."

There are some great men out there who were born into bad conditions. A lot of great men who have tremendous potential and the ability, the skill set, but they come out of very harsh environments. Lots of us with that kind of background are not taught how to be gentle, caring, and considerate, and we have to learn that in order to experience loving and lasting relationships.

FANTASIA

Lots of men are taught to be strong, be hard, and so Kendall carried that for a lot of years in his life.

KENDALL

The paradigm of manhood is very broad, though. You also have men who grew up with great fathers, saw their father love their mother, saw him treat her right. Most go on to become caring men and responsible fathers. A lot of Black dads are really doing it, but they often get overlooked because we hear so much about fathers not being there. The vast majority of Black men make sacrifices so that their kids can have what they need. Most of these men I've seen try to do right. There's a lot of research that shows that Black males are the most hands-on dads of any fathers.[2] There are some phenomenal guys out there, the good guys who don't always get recognized. The nice guys who finish last, as they say. Those are big facts, all caps.

But because too many men don't have the types of positive role models my wife had as a woman, many of us have no clue about how to interact with a woman in a healthy way. I haven't always known how myself so I've had to learn and I am still learning; I'm in good company. There's a whole generation of fatherless men who have no clear understanding of the importance and purpose of contributing to breaking the very cycles that were imposed on us. There's an expectation that they will enter a relationship automatically being compassionate and engaging in give-and-take. Many of us with that background are not taught how to be gentle to a woman's needs while maintaining our masculine strength, and we have to learn that. A lot of men still think, *As long as I work, and I'm not cheating, and I help pay the bills or pay all the bills, then I'm good to go.* They don't know about opening up their emotional chambers to receive their wives, so they struggle when it comes to matters of the heart.

I think it takes a certain kind of woman to love men like me who come out of harsh conditions. I also think it requires men like us to reach a season in our lives where we have the desire within ourselves to want to change. He's got to want her so bad that he's willing to revisit everything he believes is true in order to make room for her wants and needs. When men are not willing to do that, women don't stand a chance; relationships don't stand a chance. You get conflict, you get the fighting, you get the heartbreak, so on and so forth.

---

2. Saeed Richardson, "Breaking Myths about Black Fatherhood This Father's Day," June 13, 2019, *Chicago Reporter*, https://www.chicagoreporter.com/breaking-myths-about -black-fatherhood-this-fathers-day/.

In my marriage, I had to really sit back and say, "Yo, am I really willing to revisit my perspectives and truths and even how I see myself? 'Cause how I see myself will determine my expectations for my life and my relationship and it also shapes how I see others." I have had to change the way that I see myself in order to make room for my wife as we became one and now share in a single spirit of identity before God.

KENDALL'S FAVORITE PERSONAL DEVELOPMENT BOOKS

Here are a few of the books that have helped me most in becoming the righteous man I always wanted to be:

- The Bible
- *The Masculine Journey: Understanding the Six Stages of Manhood,* by Robert Hicks
- *Outliers: The Story of Success,* by Malcolm Gladwell
- *As a Man Thinketh,* by James Allen
- *Understanding the Purpose and Power of Men,* by Myles Munroe
- *Healing the Masculine Soul,* by Gordon Dalbey

Tap In So You Don't Tap Out

KENDALL

A successful marriage or relationship takes a lot more work than many people think, and you have to build resources around you to increase your chances of success. For me, I've had to build a circle of powerful men at my roundtable who are all striving to obtain a status of elite manhood. In my circle, all my brothers are either married, engaged, or in a serious relationship. I don't have any partyers in my cirle; however, everybody's dynamic is different. We have to help each other navigate the world we face. Women are more outspoken than the previous generations of women were. They have their own destinies, their own money, their own businesses. The whole dynamic of relationships has changed. Women today compete with men in ways they didn't in the past. This means that we men must revisit the drawing board of understanding and reconsider our approach to courtship, romance, partnership, and leadership. When we do this with an open mind and a humble heart we then can make the necessary upgrades where they are needed.

FANTASIA

Pretty much! We women aren't willing to let men dominate us like some of the men did in previous generations. Those days are done. Times have really, really, really changed and our relationships have to change with them.

Sometimes one person still has in their mind-set, "Well, this is how they do it in the Bible," but the other person is saying, "Well, we gotta create a new rhythm because that time has come and gone." I think a lot of people have these conversations and arguments. I recall conversations with women who would speak of how men would say certain things to their women, talking about marriage in a whole other part of the world. We'd be like, "Maybe that's true but we are not over there—you can't have five or ten wives in America!"

A strong relationship requires a lot of discipline and practice. Lots of times we don't want to talk about discipline; we just want to experience the end result. When an artist performs in a concert, people want to hear the finished song, the crazy run or the high note the singer hits at the end. But what they don't know is how much work it took to make things appear flawless and effortless for their enter-tainment. By the time the world saw me on *Idol* I was nineteen, but I had been training for almost fifteen years. When you practice, you develop skills that allow you to do things you couldn't do before. You see the result of that discipline every time I sing. And I take that work ethic into every situation I experience, including into my marriage. You can too.

This is another place where having a relationship with God can help. 'Cause as you run into difficult issues, you cannot just rub a bottle and expect a genie to come out. You just have to fight and push through. Everybody in the Bible had a story about things they had to fight for. Find a biblical character who inspires you. Think back on the challenges you've had in your life. What did you learn? You can draw on that power in your relationship or marriage. Rather than tapping out when the going gets tough, start putting on your boxing gloves and get into the ring. Not to fight *with* each other, but *for* each other. Get used to the fight, but figure out and strategize what lessons you can use from your past and how you can make it a little easier than it was the day before.

We thank God for all of those men and women that have been placed in our lives and who have "been there and done that," because they always send us to the Good Book. I promise you that when you let Scripture lead you, your marriage will grow and doors will open. Doors have been opening for us left and right because we have not lost our faith or compromised into the model that the world may expect us to become. Even though every day isn't "peachy-cream" in our relationship, we still just keep our eyes focused on Him. That is my thing and somebody might say, "Well, that is not good enough," but that is all I got. And God is all you'll ever need.

When Less Is More

FANTASIA

One thing that can happen when we don't have real-world role models is we can spend too much time comparing ourselves to people on social media and looking to them for how our lives, or marriages, or relationships should be.

Be careful about looking at social media for role models because it gives you the illusion of perfection. It's also full of celebrities trying to make everybody believe that they are this and that. But can you even keep up with the number of celebrity breakups, filings for separations, and actual divorces that take place each year? From those who have been together for a few years to those who have been together for almost thirty years, they are dropping like flies. Think about that the next time you idolize what another couple appears to have. You would be surprised who is living large on Instagram but is broke in real life. You would be surprised who doesn't have what they say they have. Lots of people you see in the public eye, they're leasing those cars; they're renting their jewelry for the video. Many are coping with drugs and alcohol, and a lot of the most powerful people according to worldly standards are miserable inside of all their luxuries. You have public figures who've been divorced for two years, but their friends and family do not know because they are too scared to tell them because they do not want anyone to say negative things about them or for it to impact their brand. Lots of times celebrities have what we like to call "happy fake faces." They seem happy, but none of it's real.

We are living in a society where everything is quick, fast, instant, and now. People seem to blow up overnight, but in reality that rarely happens. People leave their relationships when they see the first thing they don't like: "It's over and I want a divorce." It seems like nobody wants to put in the work.

KENDALL

Always remember that on social media, everyone has filters, facades, and all sorts of nonsense. Fewer and fewer people want to be authentic anymore. I think it's important for us to take our authenticity back. I think too many of us either don't have role models, or we have lost our role models and replaced them with false idols who don't want to show any sign of weakness, loss, or struggle. Our imperfections reaffirm that we are simply human and to appear to have none is an attempt to portray gods.

To give you an example, as fathers I think we have to start raising our sons in real life and in real time—especially those of us who didn't have a father in our lives. Not everyone knows how to or feels motivated to be a role model for someone to look up to all the time. Why not share that, too, like I did when I slept on the floor with my son? Too many times, we as men do not allow our sons to see our vulnerabilities or our weaknesses, and so they don't see our imperfections and grow up knowing to express masculinity only in an aggressive manner or toxic manner when they cannot attain perfection. How beautiful would it be to say, "Son, I am just stressed out right now. I got a lot of pressure that is on me and it is not about you, but I will pull through this thing because I will do it for you. I honestly don't know how to make this work, but I will trust God to bring me on the other side." From seeing me humbled on the ground, my son watched me build my business. I don't have a college degree; matter of fact, I don't even have a high school diploma. But my son went to college. He would come home on breaks and work at my company during the summer. My lack of educational certification never hindered him from seeking me for advice and wisdom that his professors could not provide.

If you're a dad who's struggling—and we all are in one way or another—let your son watch you rise like a phoenix from the ashes. Even when you do not feel great, let him see who you really are, so he will know not to cop out, quit, and abort the mission every time something does not go his way because the only things you showed him were your successes. Show him what it is like to have pain, anger, frustration, and silence, so he will know how to process those feelings when he goes through them as a man, like all of us men have to do.

FANTASIA

What Ken has accomplished is so dope. His story is part of why I fell in love with him.

Sometimes I sit and listen to women talking about men and I hear things like, "He's got to have good credit; he's got to have this type of car; he's got to have such and such job." I find myself wanting to say, "Well, girl, you will never be in a relationship, because we are all flawed people who have been through certain things, Plus, those material standards you are demanding may come with hidden costs."

Before I met Ken, I was a queen in the making. But along the way, I was also a very depressed teenager who had battled years of insecurities. Over time, I came to realize that those insecurities that I carried were rooted in trying to meet the expectations of others instead of living my life in my own rhythm. I went through the fiery furnace and came out pure as gold. Because I went through all the things I went through, I was able to see the greatness in Ken even though he was a work in progress too. I saw the king in him. Lots of people miss out on a great relationship because they are too busy trying to put together a list of perfect things. But while you are so busy looking for all that perfect stuff, great people are passing you by.

I think that one of the problems in a lot of relationships is— everybody is chasing perfection. But a part of the reason so many fans follow me is because for the most part, I've never tried to be something I'm not. Lots of times people say to me, "How did you make it through" this and that situation? Do you know how I sleep so well at night? Because I do not want to be perfect and I do not want to make people think I am. A lot of things are out in the media about me, but nine times out of ten I shared the information myself. I gave you the information, so you cannot hold anything over me to try to embarrass me. I am allowing myself just to be human. There are people who are stuck in the past, who want to try to keep me back in my past, not understanding that I have been long gone from that. I am so far into my future.

I have never felt like I could not be myself. I take my shoes off; I am country; I tell people what I eat when I eat, when I am hungry; I make songs about it. I had a song about it on my first album that said, "This is me." So I am straight-straight. From our first date, I took the risk of telling Kendall who I really was and he told me who he was as well. And now, I sit around sometimes and think about some of the things that went on in my life and I am like, "Dang! You made it through some stuff, girl—and now you're in a marriage you didn't even dream of." Shout-out to God!

We all are human and we all are flawed. When you get to a point where you embrace your flaws and embrace and accept the things you have been through and allow them to make you a better person, you can keep going and bless someone else and say, "I have been there before. Get up and let me show you how you can also get through it. I have been through this and it left me with this scar. Where you are right now, I was there a year ago but look at me now. And a year from now you will look totally different as well." You can also accept the mistakes that another person has made and see the promise in them in spite of their scars because we all carry them. It can free you.

KENDALL

Salute to my Queen!

I think that the rat race, the constant pursuit of perfection, the pursuit of more, the insatiable appetite, the success gluttony in our society, all can cause us to miss out on the simplicity of the joys of companionship, communication, romance, and quality time. Marriage is threatened because some of us never had role models and others of us have followed worldly success and have lost track of what marriage is supposed to be about.

In our society, what you had yesterday isn't good enough today. So many of us are always searching for the next, the new, the latest version, the most recent. We may just be buying something new or upgrading our technology, but I believe our minds are being reconditioned so that we no longer appreciate the timeless, antique, and vintage traditions like marriage. We're losing the ability to appreciate the now, the moment, and still value and feel sentimental about things that were true yesterday. Instead, we seem to feel like tomorrow we need something else in order to be satisfied.

In addition to helping teens connect with each other, we know that social media are contributing to the increase in teen depression, anxiety, and suicide,[3] and undermining the family dynamic. And we would be naive to think that if everybody at the kitchen table is on their devices and in a completely different world, that it does not also pollute the simplicity and essence of a genuine relationship and marriage. The marriage is not protected because it's not compartmentalized and walled off from society. The same forces that are causing kids to lose their self-esteem are also bleeding over to relationships and marriages because our senses of identity are constantly being threatened due to social engineering.

---

3. "Teens and Social Media Use: What's the Impact?," December 21, 2019, Mayo Clinic, https://www.mayoclinic.org/healthy-lifestyle/tween-and-teen-health/in-depth/teens-and-social-media-use/art-20474437.

THE TAYLORS

We realize everyone's family situation is different. Some people don't have role models; other people do. Especially if you don't have enough role models to follow, the following exercises can help you develop the skills and confidence so that you, too, can have a strong relationship, whether you're surrounded by good examples or not:

- First, identify the parts of yourself that you like the most and areas where you are strong. What are those good characteristics? What are your strengths? Spend some time thinking about how you can bring a strength that you have in one area of your life into another, just like Fantasia brings her work ethic as a performer and Kendall brings his business skills into our marriage.

- Take a few weeks to look for people in your family, neighborhood, place of worship, community leaders, local businesses, and so on who you think highly of. Reach out to as many as you can and ask to have a conversation with them. Tell them what you admire about them and ask if they will share some stories about their path in life, the adversity they fought through, and some mentoring advice. Don't feel discouraged if some people are too busy or point you to someone else on their staff. Learn what you can from whoever you can. There are many people to admire and lots of people can help you grow.

- Considering television, YouTube, the movies, books, and social media, think about what role models stand out to you. Don't forget that in the cases of real-life public figures, filters make them look more successful in all aspects of their lives than they probably are. Nevertheless, what is it about their public persona that you like? Make a list of all the characteristics. Then journal about what you like about those characteristics and how you can practice them in your own life. Since we often admire in other people qualities that we also have within ourselves, give some thought to how those characteristics exist in you and what you can do to develop them in your relationship or marriage, or to prepare yourself for a relationship or marriage.

- Whether you are afraid to get hurt, don't have an open heart, or are addicted to your cell phone, create a list of behaviors that make it harder for you to have a relationship. When those issues come up, take some deep breaths, count to 10, pray, walk away, or do whatever you need to do to practice behaving differently.

CHAPTER 5

CALL-WAITING
Clearing the Line for Strong Communication

FANTASIA

Way back in 2013, I got a call from people representing the world-famous opera singer Andrea Bocelli. He was going to be touring the United States and wanted to know if I would sing with him. I was like, "Opera?? Whaaat!! Do they even know who they're calling?" But this was an honor—and I strongly believe in taking new challenges and developing yourself, so you don't stay stuck. So of course, I said yes!

Now, I have shared stages with a lot of people I didn't know, and I have shared stages with some of the greats—Aretha, Chaka Khan, Stevie Wonder, I could go on and on. Most of the time we have something in common—they are either of my same culture as an African

American, or they are at least an American—so I'm familiar with their background and genre. But opera? That was totally new. Plus, Andrea Bocelli is Italian and sings in Italian; I speak only English, so that was new too. But what made the experience even more challenging for me was that Andrea Bocelli lost his sight when he was twelve so I couldn't use visual cues to communicate with him. I had worked with Stevie Wonder before, so I had a little bit of experience working with a blind musician. But I knew that this experience would stretch me way outside of my comfort zone because we were different in cultures, genres, languages, and abilities.

A week or two before the tour began, Andrea sent his musical director—his MD—to rehearse with me. I had no idea what his MD was singing about as he played the piano and shared the songs we were going to sing. Were the songs about love? Were they about death? I didn't know, but on another level, I didn't need to know. I'm a deep feeler. I could watch how he was expressing himself at the piano, hear the sounds and feel the vibrations to pick up how he was feeling. I knew that I needed to sing with deep emotion.

At first it was weird to sing operatically. I was like, "Uhhh…" I also wondered if I was bringing too much of my R & B and gospel backgrounds.

"Do I sound too soulful?" I kept asking his MD.

"We don't want you to be Andrea," his MD would tell me. "Andrea wants you to be you."

I tried to feel around for the line between exploring this new style of music and removing so much of the soul and the church from my voice that I'd lose the "me" they were looking for. I also had to learn how to pronounce the words. I'm from the country; I'm slang. But I felt my way through and figured out where to put the feeling. After I got comfortable outside of my comfort zone, I figured out how to share my gift in this genre.

Then the time came to rehearse in person. This was my first time being accompanied by a full orchestra—there were more than one hundred musicians. Lots of people were speaking Italian. Sometimes as we walked through the halls together, I wondered, *Are they talking about me?* I also noticed that the opera singers' body posture was different from mine, very formal and erect. Watching them made me walk through the hallways differently. There were times when I felt so nervous. It was a totally different atmosphere.

I'm already a touchy-feely bubbly spirit and, like a lot of Black people, I'm a hugger. So when the moment came to meet Andrea, I felt comfortable when he asked to touch my hands. I can't remember quite what he said, but by touching and rubbing my hands and fingers, he could tell all sorts of things—how my face was structured, the size of my lips, things about my skin. It was like, "Whoa! Ain't no way you just told me all that and you're blind!" Even without vision, he could see who I was. Feeling me helped him see me! It was super amazing! He made me feel so comfortable that I felt like I belonged. *He invited me here*, I reminded myself. *He knows who I am. He knows what he's getting.*

As we stood in front of audiences at places like the Hollywood Bowl in Los Angeles and the Prudential Center in Newark, outside of New York City, I could tell that Andrea's fans loved him deeply. They would hear the first few notes of "The Prayer" or other very popular songs and start clapping because they had been waiting to hear them. I didn't want to butcher the experience they'd come for.

I learned that even though I was new to the genre and didn't understand the words, by leaning into my emotions real strong, I could connect with them and convey the meaning anyway. We received standing ovations and people whistled their approval in the way that opera audiences do. I could feel and see that they were experiencing an overload of emotions. And every now and then, I would give them some church, some gospel, give them me—not overkill, but to adapt my gift to a new audience looking to hear his work in a new way. And I could see the crowd's faces and watch them be like, "Wow!"

Let There Be Room for Two Perspectives

FANTASIA

How do you communicate in a heartfelt way with someone you don't really know? How do you get through to another person when you're way out of your comfort zone and sometimes they seem to speak a different language from you?

Because we got married so quickly and were still learning about each other, Ken and I had a lot to learn about how to express ourselves most effectively. We each had to communicate our part. Sometimes we hit all the same notes, but lots of times we were pitchy or clashing. We had to learn how to transmit our feelings in a way that worked for the other and listen to each other carefully.

Little did I know how much I'd learned from my experience with Andrea Bocelli and how much that had prepared me to communicate with Ken. I learned I could work with someone who sang a style far outside of my comfort zone, came from a different culture, didn't speak my language, and couldn't see me with his physical eyes, and still, we could find a common language so that we could communicate with each other. If I could do that with him, I should be able to do that with my mate. In fact, sometimes I say Ken is my Andrea Bocelli because he could see who I am without first knowing me as the rest of the world does.

Andrea and I sang a lot of duets. In music, a duet is a song with two performers. They may sing different words, different notes, and even different rhythms, but they come together to sing the lyrics in a way that is pleasing to the listener's ear. Sometimes the singers are speaking to God, as Andrea and I did in "The Prayer" and gospel singers do. Other times they're having a conversation or telling a story, like Aretha Franklin and I did in "Put You Up on Game." Then again, there are times when the singers are arguing, like Jennifer Hudson and I did in "I'm His Only Woman." In each of these songs we alternated our verses. But there is always a point in a duet where the singers sing the same words and sometimes even sing the same note at the same time.

You each contribute your part, you find your own notes, you listen carefully to try to create harmony, and you know your partner's range. This all helps you create a beautiful song that you couldn't create with your voice alone. Communicating your true emotions and finding the notes that blend harmoniously is a lot like what happens in a relationship.

KENDALL

Good communication always begins with two perspectives, whether it's a friendship, a marriage, or any other relationship. Anytime you have more than one person, you are going to have more than one viewpoint. It's important to make sure you are an active listener and communicate your part in a way that allows the other person to hear your heart in the midst of your other emotions; and keep your voice in your partner's range.

FANTASIA

Andrea and I came at things from entirely different angles. He sings tenor and I sing soprano. He sings opera; I'm a soul singer. We speak different languages. But he heard something in me that he thought would mesh well with his voice and bring something fresh to his body of work and his genre. I learned music I'd never imagined singing because I wanted to grow and have new experiences. Both of us stretched out of our comfort zone so we could reach for the emotional understanding that audiences all over the country could experience.

KENDALL

The beauty manifests when two people strive to comprehend each other. My wife doesn't have to change her perspective on anything, nor do I have to change mine. We don't change the core of who we are, but we figure out where that line of understanding is. That's when the beauty takes place.

FANTASIA

The high point of a duet occurs when the singers sing the same verse together, reach for the emotional understanding, and maybe even hit the same note, even though it may be in our own octaves. You can come together as a duo and create harmony even as you communicate differently.

Make a Deposit

KENDALL

At the bank, you cannot make a withdrawal if you have not made a deposit. In matters of the heart, you cannot expect your partner to give you something if you have not filled them up with what they need and desire.

Minister and writer Gary Chapman talks about the love languages couples use to communicate in a relationship. He has identified five different types of behavior that tend to make people feel loved:

(1) having their partner speak affirming words to them; (2) spending quality time together; (3) receiving gifts; (4) having their partner perform acts of service for them; and (5) physical touch. Chapman says that every person is different, and even though we may feel loved when our partner does some or all of these things, most of us tend to have a language or two that we're stronger at giving and a language or two that make us feel more loved when we're receiving. Sometimes people intend to be loving, but the way they show love isn't the way that feels best to their partner.[1] Misunderstandings are incredible opportunities.

For us, words of affirmation and touch are important, so my Queen and I start first thing in the morning by communicating our love and appreciation of each other. When we wake up, the first thing I do is kiss her, and tell her I love her, and remind her how beautiful she is. We are also very touchy-feely. Every time I walk past my wife, I'm touching something. I think that when one partner gives a hug, or smiles, or blushes, or whatever, those are deposits that you put into each other. Then you have something to withdraw from when one of your emotional accounts finds itself in the negative.

FANTASIA

I have always been a hugger and a touchy-feely person, and I think this is very important in a marriage. Even if Ken is just playing on his phone, I may touch his hand or his head when I walk by. We communicate with our words and with actions. We call each other King and Queen. He gives me beautiful cards that he customizes with his own words. He manages our businesses to ensure we have provision, but also as a form of protecting me from industry harm. I leave my crown on the stage and immediately turn back into his wife right

---

1. "What Are the 5 Love Languages?," 5lovelanguages.com, https://www.5lovelanguages.com/5-love-languages/.

after the show. I go to the grocery store for us. I cook for my husband and family. We love and raise our children together. We do these types of things to help communicate love.

But to know how to communicate with your partner in the best way, you have to study them just like you study for work or for school. It's like when I'm performing with another singer, I try to figure out what sounds they like to make, where their body is probably gonna go next. I look for the pocket, so our notes don't clash and to make sure my movements complement theirs.

The more I study Kendall, the more I understand and figure out how to better communicate with him. When we first met, I thought I understood a Black man with tattoos. But as I started getting to know him, I was like, "Wait a minute, this is different!" I'd never met a man who reads all the time; who reads so much that he needs reading glasses; who spends his days studying. That was new to me. I was like, "Oh shoot, he wears his tattoos totally different!" It took a while to find the pocket, like singing in a new genre.

Even seven years into my relationship with Ken, I am still learning how to communicate with him. Where is the pocket so I can complement him in a particular moment? When should I move forward with my conversation and when should I fall back? How do I not talk over him? How do we keep our notes from clashing? When should we sing the same words? When can we sing the same note in our own octaves? These are some of the things that I consider.

So study and get to know your partner. Ask them what makes them feel loved. Listen to what they're saying, wait your turn, find the right moment, practice communicating over and over, and as a couple figure out how to blend.

Active Listening

KENDALL

In any marriage or relationship, it's also important to be an active listener. Someone who listens with all their senses, focuses on the person who's speaking, lets them know through their verbal and non-verbal language—things like head nods, saying, "Um-hmm," looking them in the eye, holding their hand, and so on—that they're truly trying to understand, don't judge them, and will respond to the things that the speaker tells them.

In the beginning we struggled with this a lot. There were times when we waited for the other to take a breath just so we could hit them with our side of the argument—and every blue moon we may still do that. But an active listener doesn't just wait to make their point so they can "win." They try to create a "win" for the relationship that also works for them as an individual.

Onstage, my wife is the perfect example of active listening. One thing I've always found amazing is how she's remembering and communicating her lyrics and her chords and, at the same time, she's also listening through her in-ear monitors to the band. She's singing, but she's also looking at and communicating with the crowd; she's catching the audience's mood and improvising her notes; she's doing her steps and her routines—moving her shoulders, her hips, her feet with the beat. But all at the same time, she's hearing everything else—the beat Joy is playing on the drums, Roxy's riff on the bass, the lick that Ari's playing on the guitar. She listens not just with her ears but with her entire body and spirit—her eyes, her hips, her feet, her soul. She's doing several things at the same time and not missing anything. She improvises based on how she feels, what she sees, what she hears, and what her intuition tells her. And her band and the crowd feed off of her.

We have grown in our ability to be active listeners. When you watch us on *Taylor Talks*, you hear my Queen say things like, "Come on, now!"; or "You killed it"; or "Shut up, Ken!"; or "Big ups." Or I will say things like, "Salute"; or "Facts"; or "Bet!"; or "You hit it on the head." This is us actively listening.

FANTASIA

Being an active listener means that you have to stay open so that you can respond to what you hear. Sometimes that means you may need to go faster, go slower, find the groove, or move into the pocket—you may even need to operate outside of your main genre of communication.

On *Idol*, they want the contestants to sing different styles of music. I could have said, "I don't do different genres," but you're singing in front of the whole wide world, so again, you gotta pick songs that can communicate with everyone. My versatility allowed me to connect with sixty-four million people; that's one of the reasons why I won. Over the years, I have run into artists who say, "I don't sing that; this is what I do." And you know what happens? I see them performing at one event, but then I never see them at any others. To be successful as a singer, you have to challenge yourself to sing across the board when it comes to your music, your gift. Otherwise, you will get left at that first event and never invited back again and wonder why. I think this is true across many aspects of life. It's definitely necessary when it comes to relationships. Relationships challenge you to journey off into different rhythms, and sounds, and instruments than you're used to.

As I've listened to Ken, I've learned that there are certain "sounds" and "songs" that he likes. I could say, "I don't sing that kind of music," but then I wouldn't meet an important need of his. When he likes certain things, I try to keep doing them. But as each chapter of our marriage unfolds, I find that I may need to adjust and sing differently. I sang one kind of song when we were just newlyweds. I needed to switch up when we went into business together. Now that we have a baby, we need to move in an entirely different tempo. Relationships and marriage aren't one way all the time. Each partner moves through seasons. We need to adjust. When I do my part well, I can feel the good energy in our relationship and our home real strong. When the energy goes a little off, maybe I gotta shift to smooth jazz from rock soul. My family is my ultimate crowd, and I desire to win their hearts and happiness with my performance as a wife and mother as well.

Prepping and Plating

KENDALL

We've also learned that how we serve up what we have to say is very important. My wife and I, we like to go out to eat. We go to certain restaurants because we love the food. But the food isn't always what makes the difference. How does the restaurant prep and plate the food for us? Some restaurants make a big production of serving you so that the food seems more special. Others present food on the plate like it's a work of art. Is it slopped onto the plate like some instant mashed potatoes or does it have a pat of butter, some fresh pepper, and decorative parsley on top? That helps distinguish the best restaurants from the good ones.

I've learned that I want Fantasia to "plate" her conversation with me the same way I see her "plate" it for the world—thoughtfully, kindly, and sensitively—and she wants the same thing from me. Sometimes we have a disconnect when maybe silently I expect a certain plating and packaging or she expects certain plating and packaging, and the other person just slops it on the plate like some box mac 'n' cheese. We're learning that many times when that happens it's because we're feeling pressure from the industry or other entities outside of our marriage that's bleeding impatience into how we interact with each other. But just as in any restaurant, you can't allow the pressure from a rush of customers to impact the level of service you are known for.

FANTASIA

Every singer has a range of sound where their voice is most comfortable. Some singers are high-pitched (soprano), and at the other end there's deep and commanding (bass). Alto, tenor, and baritone fall in between. When you communicate, it's important to use the right tone—one that's appropriate for the occasion and makes your partner feel most comfortable.

Take the time to study your partner so you can figure out what sounds are most soothing to his or her ear. Compare the sound of your voice to how some of their favorite vocalists sound, both when you're speaking normally and if you are raising your voice. As you listen to the different vocal ranges, pay attention to the feelings they produce in your body and spirit, then make adjustments as necessary.

It also makes a difference how a note is sung. Even if I'm singing the same notes, my husband will respond differently to me depending on how I deliver them. If I communicate in a more powerhouse, belt-it-out or a very rowdy-rowdy tone—like the parts of my show when I get buck wild and start rocking my head back and forth—that hits him differently than if I express myself in loving and peaceful Nancy Wilson or Dinah Washington sounds or give him the graceful Fantasia who accompanied Andrea Bocelli. It's easier for him to receive what I say if I sing like Nancy, Dinah, or Andrea, so I try to keep my communication at a volume and tempo that feel comfortable to him. Over the years, I've learned how important it is to make sure I'm communicating in a way that doesn't sound screechy or harsh—or make the microphone scream, or hum, or whistle, or blow out the amp. I want my messages to harmonize so Kendall can hear my song, and feel it, and know that what I'm expressing is true.

I've learned that sometimes we women need to watch when and how much we use our soprano—our high-pitched voice. I know I have been guilty of that. When we're in a spat, those notes are too high for him. I need to be able to say, "Okay, wrong key, girl," then deliver what I have to say in my alto or tenor voice. A man may need to turn down the bass, so it doesn't make the room vibrate, or overwhelm our song, or even scare us.

KENDALL

When emotions flare—or insecurities rise in either of us, or maybe unspoken expectations aren't met—they start to pollute the delivery, and the delivery causes the message to get lost.

Shifting Our Atmosphere

KENDALL

My wife has taught me how to intentionally create peaceful energy in our relationship and home. I didn't know this was possible until I met her, but we do it. For us, that process starts with prayer. Both of us have always been very much into prayer, and as a couple we are into it even more. I used to pray and let it go, but now I'm also into meditation. Meditation is important because sometimes we pray and immediately jump right back into the same things we were doing before we started praying. But it's important to be still so you can listen for God's answer or the comfort of His Holy Spirit. The Most

High can speak to you in many ways—whether in words, or an idea that pops into your head, or you might sense something intuitive. Meditating helps to keep our home and marriage peaceful.

The sounds, colors, shapes, and fragrances we pick out for our home help us keep that vibration so we stay grounded and centered. Before I met my wife, I played rap nonstop. I didn't care where I was at, who I was with, whatever. But I've learned that if you're in a relationship and listening to rap all the time, you're not doing anything with your conscious and subconscious mind to promote what you truly want to output in that relationship. Listening to the news or listening to rap music creates a certain negative messaging in my subconscious that I don't want while I'm with my wife. When I played rap all the time, I was always intense; I was always short-tempered, shortsighted. Subconsciously, lots of times it's getting you ready for a fight. Plus, my mind moves too much and I can get anxious, so I try to stay calm. So now all I play in my office is meditative music, jazz, because it allows me to get focused and stay focused. Mood music helps me stay calm but still motivated. Before he died, XXXTentacion talked about the power of sonic waves to change moods and send messages. So I also tune in to YouTube to find things that allow me to really tap into my right brain and my left brain, my creative side and my intellect. It is almost impossible to keep the lines of communication clear when the mind is congested with bumper-to-bumper traffic of negative and harmful influences.

FANTASIA

I'm always tickled when I hear Ken listening to meditation music. Music has the power to shift people's energy. People don't usually think about it this way, but there's energy coming from all of the different sounds—the band, the soloist, the background singers, the choir, and even the crowd singing along. I mean, who hasn't had an experience when they've walked into a room and the energy was off. When the room felt a little dark, a little cloudy, a little gray-looking based on something that happened before you got there. No matter your mood, music can help shift it. I play a lot of instrumentals because I like a room to feel bright and sunny.

KENDALL

My wife is into taking baths, using aromatherapy and playing spa music. Before her, I didn't know how much I liked those things, but now I also do them for myself. That's right, fellas, a relaxing bath and smooth sounds do wonders for this ex–street cat. Tattoos and bubbles!

FANTASIA

There is power in aromatherapy—how the smell of a rose, or of lavender, or even of eucalyptus can just change your mood in a minute. I want our house to have the fragrance of happiness, joy, and good energy. So we burn incense and oils a lot. I like it when I smell Ken burning frankincense and myrrh sticks.

Paying attention to energy has just been dope for our household and keeps our communication strong.

KENDALL

As the husband of a world-famous vocalist, you would think that I would always get to hear her sing. But Fantasia gets too nervous to sing to me. The only time I hear her singing is when I hear her in a different room in the house and I creep up close and just vibe without her knowing I'm there.

FANTASIA

I do not get nervous. I just think it is corny. Come on, can you imagine you just wake up and I am in the shower vocalizing?

KENDALL

I wish you would! My life is like being a rancher who has twenty thousand cows, but you cannot get one glass of milk.

THE TAYLORS

As you learn your partner and study their energy, you get better at singing your song in the right key. Keep a mental list of songs; then imagine what song in your catalog best expresses what you want to communicate in any given moment. Is it some "summertime and the living is easy"? Is it "rock with you"? Stack your mental playlist so you play the right song to create the right mood with your partner, at the right time.

CHAPTER 6

ESCAPE ROOM
Handling Emotional Conflict

FANTASIA

At this point in our relationship, we don't argue very much. We have found security in being able to lovingly disagree. But we got into a little spat about eight months into COVID that we wanted to share with you in hopes that our transparency will reveal that agreement at times can begin from moments of innocent confusion. When love is allowed to rule, harmony can be reclaimed time and time again.

COVID affected everybody differently. The music industry shut down and I couldn't tour. We knew lots of people who got laid off, or their business closed, or the industry flatlined and they didn't have the financial cushion to cover themselves. We also knew quite a few people who got sick and even a couple who lost their lives. We would say special prayers for them and their families. In spite of all the negativity that COVID has brought to the world, I still tried to find light at the end of the tunnel. After seventeen straight years of touring, I'd been praying, "God, I'm tired. I need a break."

We had also been trying to get pregnant for about three years. It turned out that one of my tubes was closed. At a certain point we just decided to fall back from all the pregnancy apps and things and turn it over to God. But then one day I woke up like, "Something's different..." We were blessed to be pregnant with a little girl and decided to name her Keziah, a name that I saw in the book of Job. Keziah London, we decided to name her. But by then I was thirty-six and so pregnancy was higher risk. I promised myself that I would do whatever I needed to give this baby the best possible start. For once, I would get a chance to take care of my baby and me while I was pregnant.

KENDALL

In the meantime, we didn't know how long the pandemic was gonna last, and as a husband I wasn't going to sit on my heels and wait to see how bad it was gonna get. I had to make sure that my family was protected. So, each day I blocked out from nine in the morning to anywhere between 4:00 and 6:00 p.m. to take care of business for my family. I worked from home, but I demonstrated a mental discipline that I was going into the office. I also made sure to have a cutoff time, so that I was not absent from my family.

FANTASIA

On one level, I was grateful to have Ken to cover us, but after a while I started feeling hurt because it seemed like he was always busy. For once, I finally had the chance to slow down enough to appreciate my pregnancy and to go through it with a partner. I wanted to share the experience with Ken. But every time I asked for his time—whether it was just to ride to Target, or to go to the grocery store, or to watch *Housewives*, or whatever—he was too busy or too tired. We had a little spat or two. I told him that I was feeling overlooked and neglected. He told me that sometimes he felt like I didn't appreciate the way he was fighting for our family financially. We shared our frustrations, then we looked for agreement—it turns out we both wanted to spend time together, but it was just a matter of figuring out when and how. Once we gained that understanding, we could move forward together.

KENDALL

Now that we're seven years into our marriage, it's been a long time since we've had a major fallout. The big stuff that can knock a man down? We're like, "Oh, that's nothing but Goliath. You got your slingshot?"

These days, we bump heads over the most petty, trivial things, like who's supposed to load up the dishwasher, or whether the other put enough clothes in the washing machine before running it or cutting the lights off—we fuss about silly stuff.

The Foundation

KENDALL

Every relationship or marriage will experience moments and phases when you see things differently, disagree, argue, and even fight. We are no different from anyone else, but we've learned it's important to build a strong foundation by preparing ourselves before we have disagreements, since we know we are bound to have them.

Taking steps to build a strong foundation prepares you to withstand the weight of the pressures of life. How much pressure your marriage can handle depends on how deep you build its foundation. The depth of the foundation will also determine what you can accomplish together—how high your marriage can rise. I think about the foundation of a relationship as being a lot like the foundation of a skyscraper. If you've ever seen a high-rise under construction, you know that the first thing they do is dig its basement. The basement goes down many floors. In fact, in the highest buildings the basement can be as deep as a football field. It is the depth of the basement underneath that helps to determine how high the skyscraper will be able to rise.

FANTASIA

First off, when it comes to preparing for our disagreements, we always know that we can and will get over them and reach understanding because we are God's children. Victorious people were never meant to settle for normal. So, we prepare for our spats beforehand by taking some of the steps that we've already spoken about—we study and then serve each other, speak life into each other's spirit, and pay attention when the energy shifts by asking if everything's okay and making adjustments. We do these and other things to put us on a solid foundation for the times when we disagree.

Part of the foundation that keeps me strong when I'm experiencing conflict in my life is the power of prayer. I have loved God ever since I was a little girl—I mean, I just love God. My grandmother and my mother instilled prayer in us at a young age. So, when Ken and I are hit with a lot of challenges, rather than trying to figure things out by myself or approach things my own way, my first step is to go into war through the Word and through prayer. Prayer helps. The more I grow in my faith, the more I learn that I do not have to fight all my battles myself. There are times I do not have to take any action.

Sometimes God wants me to fall back awhile. Just sit in the pocket and let Him fight for me.

KENDALL

Some of the most important work a relationship or marriage requires is for both participants to anchor themselves, the relationship, and their family in things that ground them. I'm talking about getting clear about your spiritual principles and practices, your values, your morals, your ethics, your belief systems, your paralleling purposes. Things like these help to form the basis for a strong relationship. They will strengthen you to help you deal with the stresses of life—your job, bills, car notes, rent and mortgages, the cost of your children's schooling and activities, and so on.

The "Right vs. Wrong" Myth

FANTASIA

Another important part of a strong relationship is not getting trapped in the idea of being right. Especially in the beginning of our marriage, I admit that too often I held tightly to my own plans and to the outcome that I thought should come to pass. Sometimes it was hard to let go of all the things that I had imagined for my life. There were times when I just wanted it the way I wanted it and that caused a lot of disagreements within our marriage and our business.

KENDALL

My wife is not the only one. Something like 99 percent of our disagreements have taken place because one of us was trying to establish ourselves as being right and the other person as wrong. I have been that guy, especially in the beginning. I thought I was right a lot, but I did not realize how much of a jerk I was—like, how selfish, self-centered, unmovable. It was one thing for Fantasia to think, *Oh, girl, he's got potential,* but it was another thing to get that potential to become a reality. It was like juice in an orange that has not been squeezed; it was there, but she couldn't taste it at first because she still had to shoulder all my mistakes.

FANTASIA

Today, we realize that to take care of your marriage, you have to face what you thought your life would look like and let that go. I learn a lot from watching Bishop T. D. Jakes. He says that letting go of what you already have in mind is a challenge, but life will never go exactly your way. The key when you come together with someone is to let go of what you wanted, let God do what He has planned, and then experience, understand, and expect the power that your agreement creates in your relationship. I needed to let go of what I wanted, and I needed to let go of the idea of being right. That freed us up to create something better than I could have ever imagined.

KENDALL

We've learned that the idea of right vs. wrong is a big myth, a deadly mistake rooted in selfishness. Right and wrong come into play only when facts are involved, such as in math, science, universal law, and eternal principles. There is no debate that 2 + 2 = 4. That is math; therefore, it is universally true. Not so much when it comes to matters in a relationship.

FANTASIA

Some people like rock, some people like jazz, some people like R & B. They are just different types of music. None of those choices are right or wrong, better or worse.

Especially in the beginning, we would end up fighting about who was right and wrong when we were just two people looking at the same thing differently. That meant we had to be willing to let go of control.

KENDALL

Today, we understand that rather than being right or wrong, we're just looking at things from different perspectives. Some things are absolutely true to us, but that view may not always be shared by someone else.

What we feel, need, want, and believe—all of us experience these things as our own personal truths. However, nine times out of ten, our spouse or partner has their own personal emotions, needs, and wants. In other words, they have their own perspectives. Two well-meaning people looking at the exact same thing may see it completely differently and end up fighting about right or wrong when it's not necessarily about right and wrong. It's just that something could've been done differently; something could've been done better or adjusted without error being involved.

And then there are our personal preferences: Okay, that's how I run the dishwasher or do the laundry, or that's how my mama taught me to do it. Again, neither is good or bad.

So, when people clash in a fight or a debate, the root is usually something inside themselves that causes them to try to dominate and force their way upon the other person. Since we're human, sometimes we want our partner to look, reflect, and do things the way we want them to. But our relationships will operate more smoothly if we respect the way our partner sees certain things, the way she says certain things; the way she puts the dishes in the dishwasher; the way she drives a car. It helps to learn to love those differences and stop trying to control.

Many times, the root of our conflict is that we're really at war with ourselves. What we're struggling with is not really our partner, but our own need for control, our own defense mechanisms. That's why a person can go from relationship to relationship and find themselves in the same situation over and over. You're the common denominator and you're battling over either control, perspective, or preferences. It's possible that we could both be right based on how we grew up, what we were taught, the pains we've experienced, or the expectations we have based on what we have been exposed to.

Destination: Understanding

KENDALL

The big win happens when we can win as a couple. But for two people to come into agreement, each person has got to be willing to pour at least half of their own cup out. If your cup is all the way filled to the top, your partner cannot pour any of their spirit, their gifts, their preferences, or their opinions into your glass. Not having room for your partner's perspective means you have unrealistic expectations for them and for your relationship.

FANTASIA

Letting go of what you already have in mind can be a challenge. Real talk! But the key when you come together with someone is this: you let go of what you wanted, and let God do what He has planned. When you open yourself up for that to happen you break through your limitations as an individual and experience and understand the power that develops when people come into agreement. The Bible talks about how when two or three are gathered in His name (see Matt. 18:20), and everybody's of one accord, greater things can happen than any one person could have accomplished by being right. That is true in our marriage.

KENDALL

So, instead of fighting over right and wrong, now we fight to understand each other. We prioritize walking away from disagreements with a sound appreciation of what each person needs. That way we may have two routes but only one destination: understanding. We don't have to change the core of who we are, but together we can figure out where that synergy line of understanding falls, and that's what keeps the marriage moving forward in a healthy manner. That's where the beauty takes place.

The two routes allow for our differences; the destination is what we share in common. In fact, common ground should be the only thing we fight for because it ensures we are fighting together, not fighting against each other. Rather than risk emotional clashes by continuing to force our individual opinions, we try to remove our spirit of pride and open ourselves up to the spirit of harmony. We intentionally choose to forfeit our personal agendas. Sometimes we even agree that we will disagree.

In fact, at this point in our relationship, when we are debating, lots of times I will just step out of it and say, "Babe, I apologize. I'm willing to look at it through your lens."

Because there's not always a victory in being right. I mean, what's the point of being right if it is going to keep me away from my Queen? Do I want to be right, or do I want to be close to her? If it's gonna keep me away from her, I'm wrong. I don't like to argue; I don't care nothing about it. You could be right and be sleeping alone. You could be right and not have dinner. You could be right and in a bed by yourself. Your "right" ain't always comfortable for you; it ain't gonna caress you. So, pick your poison: Do you wanna sleep and snuggle with your pride or your partner? That's really what it boils down to. You got to look at yourself. Rather than trying to be right all the time, trying to fix your mate, or getting tired of her, if you want your relationship to be healthy, get tired of yourself and fix the way you do and see things. Facts!

Don't Pull the Trigger

FANTASIA

We've also learned to treat each other with white gloves, especially when we disagree. Ken and I discovered that we can get dressed up, we can go out and interact with the people in various businesses and industries who want us on their own terms, want us to do what they want us to do. We have to figure out how to communicate, or get our point across, without growling at them. But then sometimes when we come back home, we allow some of the aggression, the bad energy, to come home with us. There are times when we don't communicate in the same way, or we're not as patient with each other as we are with people outside our home.

KENDALL

Sometimes, when you're disagreeing, it does not even matter what you say as much as how you say it. You can forfeit your entire message because you were intent on saying or doing it this way instead of lovingly delivering it. Sometimes disagreements are all about delivery, delivery, delivery. Again, when you're feeling upset, how do you put it on the plate and serve it?

FANTASIA

Studying and listening to your partner takes a lot of work so you get to know what they prefer and need. For example, it's important to learn about each other's triggers. When I say triggers, I mean things that affect your emotional state and can cause you to feel overwhelmed or distressed. Lots of times, people get triggered because of how someone else has treated them or an experience they have had in the past.[1]

We may not know what our partner went through in their childhood, with their father, with their mother, with a stranger, or with another partner. I know there are things that people have done to me that have scarred me to the point that they're still there today. I can try to be like Christ, but I'm not Christ; I'm human. I can forgive, but as hard as I try, I can't forget them. And if we're not careful about what we say and how we say it, we can hit a person's triggers and really hurt them or cause them to go off.

KENDALL

Early in our relationship, I experienced different insecurities concerning my wife. I would not play a lot of her old music because I wondered if memories of other men could have been attached to those lyrics. News flash! Men can be very insecure. We can overcompensate for our insecurities. We do not talk about them. We do not like to admit it because we hide behind toxic masculinity. But at the very end of the day, men are very emotional, especially men who were raised by single mothers.

In my work with Salute First, I see many men who don't have enough emotional strength. They are popping off; they are ready to quit; they are ready to abort the mission; they are ready to shoot and

---

1. Crystal Raypole, "What It Really Means to Be Triggered," April 25, 2019, Healthline, https://www.healthline.com/health/triggered.

take a life. They are not growing. You also have some males who are older in age but never fully became men. We have to develop more emotional strength. We cannot be so sensitive. We have to be able to manage our insecurities.

I believe the ego is like pesticide. It stunts the way that we are supposed to grow and our natural maturation process. We cannot grow if we do not allow ourselves to receive constructive criticism, especially from the people close to us. We have to get to a point where a woman can come to us and let us know what she needs, and we can't take it personally or see it as an assassination of our character. Because the people at the office, they are in the matrix. They do not see who we really are. The people out in the community where we are playing ball, they do not see who we really are. But our wives, our kids, those closest to us when we are not in the matrix—they know exactly who we are. Their feedback provides us the greatest opportunity to grow, to be better, and to improve at home and the way we navigate the matrix, because they are our real foundation and the mirror in which we can see our true reflection.

So, all of us have to be able to receive constructive criticism when it is given in love and handled with emotional intelligence, especially men. Our machoism has to take a backseat because the ego is going to prevent growth. That is your partner coming to you. That is your best friend who is not trying to hurt you or belittle you. She is trying to tell you something so you can get more of what you enjoy in abundance. If you do not handle constructive criticism correctly, you risk losing everything that is on the table in the first place.

So, take it from me and check your insecurity. Know that when she is correcting you and saying, "I'd rather go to McCormick & Schmick's instead of McDonald's," it is just because she wants to switch it up a little bit. She is not attacking your cash flow; she is not saying you are not a man. She is just saying that there is more out there. She wants to experience it with you.

Watch Your Words

KENDALL

That said, how you talk to your mate is very important. God specifically says that freshwater and salt water cannot come out of the same faucet (see James 3:11). You should not praise and worship God, but then hurt someone out of the same mouth. In fact, hurtful words shouldn't come out of your mouth at all with someone you love.

When I hurt my wife verbally, I am cutting my own wrist. If I disrespect my wife, I am disrespecting myself. If I say something that is verbally abusive, that is cowardly, especially as the head over our marriage. But I'm also human. I have had to learn that when I am emotional, and when I am hot, when I am hurt—when I find myself in one of these emotional states—I need to step back so that I don't say the first thing that comes into my head. I am not going to feel better by tearing my partner down. It's essential to build your partner up.

FANTASIA

This is still another reason why it's important to study your partner—so you understand what hurts your partner and avoid doing it. Once you hurt me, okay, I'm gonna forgive you, and we're gonna move on. But if it keeps happening, that's something else.

KENDALL

There are two sources of energy: love and fear. When I am truly rooted in love, I monitor what I do and speak life into my wife's spirit. I don't say the first thing that comes to my mind. But when we are flooded with fear—when we start manipulating, raising our voice, criticizing, name-calling, and so on—that's when we try to control. Fear drives us to want to control things so that we do not get hurt, so that we do not experience setbacks.

FANTASIA

When we're feeling fearful, it's important not to use words as weapons. But I admit that I haven't always done this well. There have been times when I've said, "Oh, Lord. God, if I say I am a King's kid and I am Your child, I cannot be talking to my husband like that." When I mess up, sometimes it is hard for me to go back to God and pray because I'm embarrassed.

KENDALL

Sometimes when we're arguing, the feelings that are in our hearts, our emotions, our traumas, get intensified. If we're not careful, we can take them out on our partner. For many couples, relationship is the one place in life where they can unlock the invisible contents of their Pandora's boxes of disappointments, hurts, frustrations, heart-breaks, and traumas. But nothing in society teaches us how to do that in a constructive way. We're almost set up for failure. Too often neither the person who owns the Pandora's box, nor the person who has the key, is knowledgeable about how to handle its contents. You may even have two Pandora's boxes open at the same time in a relationship, and the contents of both could be toxic.

FANTASIA

I've released my Pandora's box on Kendall before, and I cannot do that anymore. So, now I'm learning how to let go of all the frustrations that I have—whether it's work related, or the kids, or on and on—at different times throughout the day, so they don't build up. I don't want them to keep our relationship from going to the next level.

KENDALL

When you dump all your traumas or frustrations on your partner, you cannot expect them to be ready and prepared to handle what you have to say. Communicating has a yin and yang vibe. You must think about the delivery of what you want to say, but you also have to consider how your partner will receive it. Queen and I have learned that when we are feeling insecure and are not ready to manage our delivery we should just press pause until we feel emotionally secure. It cannot be, "I just need to get this off my heart," followed by a hurtful dump. We have to be responsible. So when your Pandora's box of emotions flies open, take a step back until you can share without lashing out. When you're upset, take some deep breaths to help calm yourself. Or take a moment to remember your wedding or your favorite song together. It helps me to meditate on how God sees my wife as fearfully, and wonderfully, and uniquely made to do what He put her here to do. That's different from the way I sometimes see her since I'm human and can be selfish. Then, once you feel ready, open your heart to your partner. Now the other person has a responsibility to reciprocate that same energy as well.

FANTASIA

I am still self-checking—making sure I am straight first—before I come to Ken with something I'm feeling frustrated about. I ask of God, "Whatever is not like You, I do not want it. If it is not something You want for me, God, take it away."

Jonathan McReynolds has a song titled "Make Room." "I will make room for you," the chorus goes. He tells God to move different things over to make room for God—his ego, his social media, his

Facebook time. He tells God to take it if it is not what He wants for him. Move it over.

So, my language, how I speak to people, how I treat people—if it is wrong, God, move it out of the way so I speak the way You would have me speak. We've got to learn how to self-check first—to make sure we are straight, then move forward from there.

Escape Room

KENDALL

Sometimes when my wife gets mad at me, I do not eat right. I already told you she has mastered the one-portion dinner. She will whip up a portion fit for a queen only. I smell it cooking, but then she takes her plate and goes into the bedroom. I can hear the door close. I am like, "Well, I either need to go in there and face her or just go ahead and befriend my couch." We have gotten much better. I don't sleep on the couch as much and she does not put the pillows between us any longer—that was our second year of marriage. Now she just sleeps on the far side of the bed, balancing like a gymnast on the balance beam—so close to the edge that if she sneezed, she would fall off. When I wake up in the morning, she is already gone even though she has nowhere to go.

Then I have to figure out some way to get her back. I look for the puzzle pieces and clues to get back in her good graces. She's not always the type who opens both doors and lets them swing wide open. Sometimes when I mess up, I have to look for a small little crack, peek through a window, look for the opportunity to get back in the door. If I was too far out of line, she might give me a peephole. Like, "Squeeze your pride through that gap so we can get our relationship back on track." Those things have to be more important than my ego and my pride. It's almost like I have to figure out the clues to an escape room, where people solve puzzles and figure out clues to get out of a room or situation before a timer runs out.

FANTASIA

When Ken and I are bumping heads, we give the other space to get away until we're able to come back together and get back on track.

KENDALL

Queen loves to go shopping when she needs to take a break from me.

FANTASIA

Yeah, well, when Ken's mad at me, he goes by himself to see the movies that we had agreed we were going to see together.

KENDALL

I don't go rush to my homeboys and put my business out in the street; I don't involve my mama. I don't turn to porn; I don't do the strip club. That's just not my character. I don't go to the bar to get drinks—because the drink is gonna lower your character and your level of consciousness and awareness, so when your old crush walks up and says, "Hey, Big Head," you're not thinking about your partner. But the one thing I will do if we get mad at each other, and she doesn't wanna speak to me, is I will go right to the AMC theater!

FANTASIA

In a marriage, our weak moments are when the work really happens. So, it's important to find ways to take some space from each other and the conflict in harmless or constructive ways so you don't get more upset. Ken and I each have our own favorite ways to back up, cool down, and center ourselves so that we don't let the world enter our home or take our frustrations out on each other. I usually talk to God, then I meditate to listen for His answers. But sometimes I'm too embarrassed to talk to Him right away. As a singer, I'm also sensitive to sound and energy, so I do things like listen to the old love songs, like Nancy, Luther, Anita Baker. I have singing bowls that make beautiful sounds that calm me. I'm gonna light my candles; I'm going to burn my sage; I have little rocks that I like to put in my hand; I put on all my energy bracelets; I'm gonna take a bath or try to be around water. I also have my favorite TV shows and I like to read a good book.

KENDALL

I keep meditation music going all the time and, as my wife and I already told you, I will go to the movies. I love to go to the gym and work out. I like my prayer time. I like reading the Bible, a self-help book, or a business book. I watch certain YouTube videos that calm my mind. I have learned that the hard times truly define a marriage, so it is critical to monitor what we do as men when we find ourselves in one of those tight spaces. That, too, will define our character and integrity as men.

FANTASIA

But it's also important to find ways to cater to each other. When your partner is upset, why not just submit, and cater to them?

When Ken's upset, I can stop our fight from escalating by asking what I can do to help make him feel happy. Is it by making him a good dinner? Is it watching MMA with him? To calm things down, these days I reach for understanding. Because while I might not agree with everything he does, I do know one thing: I love Ken. We can agree upon that.

Then we start compromising. When I'm feeling off, I promise Ken that if he just gives me an hour to shift my energy, when I come back, I will have let it go. Sometimes we find it helps to go into separate rooms and remember the first time we laid eyes on each other and our wedding day. From that energy it's easier to figure out what we each want to say and to communicate from that space. When we come back together, we're both willing to stop arguing. Now we can sit down and figure out how we can stop our little war. We can ask each other: What do we want love to look like in this house? What would make you feel better right now? What helps you after coming home from a long day at work? What helps you when you come home from the road? What can we do, babe, to help you release that?

Crack the Code

KENDALL

Matters of the heart are vulnerable territory, but who is teaching us what forgiveness looks like?

Who has ever sat you down and said, "This is how you forgive"? Many of us are not properly trained; we haven't seen it in our homes the correct way—and TV, music, all the media are not reinforcing the godly perspective. Spiritually, forgiveness is a loving and courageous invitation that gives a person another opportunity to prove that they realize their behavior, their actions, hurt the other person, and that they have learned, and are committing to never do that again. Forgiving does not mean we wipe the behavior away and act like it never happened. It is an invitation to right that wrong and to repent. Repenting means that you acknowledge what you did was wrong, you take accountability, and you turn around and try to never commit that act again.

I believe this is the way it is supposed to work: The person who is hurt, scarred, traumatized, whatever, is pushing past their pain, fear, and anxiety. They're being courageous enough to extend access to the person who caused that affliction. They're saying, "I love you so much that I'm gonna give you a ticket for another opportunity to not do that to me again."

FANTASIA

We shouldn't treat forgiveness like a demerit, like, "Okay, I'm just gonna put this on your record, and it will stay there." But this is where lots of couples mess up: "You ask me to forgive you, so I forgive you, but I'm also asking you not to do that again." But whenever we're mad and we're intense we might go back and do the same thing. We have to be careful not to allow that to happen.

KENDALL

A lot of times we get caught up in disagreements because I said something that offended my wife, but it is not something I would be offended about. The things that offend her do not necessarily offend me. If it offends her, if it upsets her, if it hurts her, then it is a problem. You have to pull that kind of stuff back. Other times we have stalemates when nobody wants to be the one to apologize first. As the head of our family, I try to lead in the forgiveness area. It's just another way of serving. When we're mad, sometimes we lose sight of the need to serve each other. But if you get back to having a serving heart, the attention will come, the affection will return, the romance will rejuvenate, and you will be in a mature place again. But it begins with serving and humility.

If your partner is upset with you, somebody has to make the first move. In the beginning of our marriage, I would be hesitant, because no man wants rejection. But I learned to be the first one to move forward. Back when we used to argue a lot, I'd try sliding a letter under the bedroom door. At first, I might see it in the trash can the next day, but then I would attempt it again until I figured out how to crack the code that would help us escape our disagreement. Know that the first time you go in, she may shoot it down, but over time I learned that it was possible to wear her down. Sometimes I felt like Don Corleone trying to make her an offer she couldn't refuse.

FANTASIA

Ladies, please, please, please, please, please, I'm begging you. Do not be like I was and stay trying to win and be right, where you are not giving him anything, and you are not cooking, you are not cleaning. That is how the enemy starts to work on your mind. Tamika from down the street says, "Hi," but then you start wondering, like, *What is going on?* when all she is doing is being a nice neighbor.

So instead of letting time go by—like those awkward minutes when you are both quiet or days or weeks when you are not speaking, and the tension just gets thicker and thicker and thicker—you have to learn how to humble yourself at that moment. I'm learning to shut it down right there. Yes, it is hard to do, but that is your soul mate; that is your husband; that is your wife; that is your partner; that is your lover. So it is best to just do it right at that time. I would rather spend the rest of the day with Ken watching Netflix and eating good food than me in one room and him in the other watching something different.

So after we have a spat, I am learning just to keep the conversation going.

"Are you good?" I'll ask him.

KENDALL

I'll tell her, "Yeah, I am good. Are you good?"

FANTASIA

"Yeah, I'm good," I'll tell him.

At this point, almost seven years in, I am learning to move on, even when we have a heated disagreement. I do not want to keep focusing on that. You can hold on to stuff, but then every argument you get into, you stay stuck in that same situation.

At this point I cannot even remember when we last fought hard, because we have been building and building so strong.

Listening for the Good Notes

FANTASIA

While we were writing this book, I realized that sometimes when Kendall and I butt heads, it's because I'm bringing my singing skills to our relationship in a way that interferes with good communication. When you reach a certain level as a singer—as an artist, as a professional—you expect that almost all the notes the choir sings, or the musicians in your band play, will be correct. A professional expects that everyone's practiced, so we all come to rehearsal knowing our parts. We stop listening for what's right and start trying to pick out the bad notes—the voice that's out of tune, the notes that are off-key. So, most of the time I'm listening for the stuff that I wanna change. I listen for what's wrong, not what's right.

I might say, "Hey, that was not the right note that you played." Or "Yo! Before you start doing dah-dah-dah, I want you to go bop-bop-bop-bop."

It dawned on me that sometimes I don't hear all the right things Kendall says. Sometimes I listen for his "bad notes." I point out only the things he says that I disagree with, or that are piercing or hurtful to me, even though most of the notes he sings are right.

KENDALL

Sometimes when she does that, I'm like, "But did you get what I'm saying?" And when the only thing she talks about or mentions is those one or two things I said that were wrong, or when she misses the message due to a few minor details, sometimes I'll say what I have to say and then just walk away. There are also times where I, too, have been guilty of nit-picking smaller portions of the message instead of allowing the overall voice of her heart to be fully heard. We do much better now, and we continue to reach for understanding beyond our difference in perspectives, not allowing insignificant points to rob us of our need for healthy communication. Just as when my wife performs, I don't think a ticket buyer would go home disappointed just because a single note was sung out of tune.

FANTASIA

I am working to recognize and change that about myself. At the same time, because I'm a musician, I hear everything; I don't miss a beat. So I actually do hear what he's saying, but I need to do a much better job of acknowledging all his good notes as well. Almost all of King's notes are really good notes.

I know I'm not the only person who does this. So when you offer feedback to your partner, make sure to acknowledge all their good notes—all the things they do right—rather than just focusing on only the things you disagree with or would like them to do differently.

And always remember the power in prayer. No matter who is wrong, allow God to show you how to go back. Ask Him to give you a makeover, a remodel, a remix. When you get that person back, then just clock in and work for it—because a relationship is work.

KENDALL

I am a firm believer that you pray, and you get back on your feet. Ask God whether you did something and need to atone for it, or you have not done anything, and you just cannot get through to that person because of style and distance. Just leave the environment in the room available for that person to come back. Give them space to process their thoughts. And if that person is not speaking or being intimate, just focus on what you are doing. Do you return dirty for dirty, or get cold and bitter and start rejecting them? Or are you still walking around with a smile? Are you still treating them well? Are you operating as the head reflecting how Christ is with His church? Patience is what you do while you wait.

And remember that love truly conquers all.

THE TAYLORS

We're not experts in relationships, so we take a few of our cues from the Gottman Institute, a nonprofit organization that specializes in relationships. They encourage couples to focus on communication. Though you may do so imperfectly, it's important to learn to listen to and understand each other, so you don't get stuck on major issues. Rather than blaming each other for things you don't like, practice using "I " statements when you communicate. For example, say, "You make me mad when you do so and so" less, and "I get mad when you do so and so" more. Also, when you have a spat, avoid cutting and criticizing your partner, expressing contempt toward them, being defensive, and stonewalling—four behaviors that are so bad for any relationship that some experts call them the Four Horsemen of the Apocalypse.[2]

We believe the best time to prepare for your disagreements is

2. Gottman Institute, https://www.gottman.com/blog/the-four-horsemen-recognizing -criticism-contempt-defensiveness-and-stonewalling/.

before they take place. So why not take some time now to place yourself on a firm foundation?

- Write out or record a prayer asking God to help you let go of an area of self-righteousness, insecurity, anxiety, unspoken expectations, or selfishness.
- If you knew that this spat would work out, and you wouldn't be feeling so strongly about it a week, a month, or a year from now, what would you do? How important would it be to win?
- Think of a disagreement you and your partner have. What is another way of looking at it? What is another way? What is another? Now, look back at your original perspective. Do you still feel as strongly about it?
- Make a list of things that trigger your partner.
- Make a list of your spouse's "good notes" and write them a card or tell them about them.

CHAPTER 7

CONTRACTS AND COVENANTS

Ties That Bind Business and Marriage

KENDALL

When Fantasia and I first met, I was in the middle of being betrayed. As I mentioned in chapter 2, in the eighteen months after I'd gotten out of jail, I'd started out working in a warehouse for $7.25 an hour. This was humbling for a twenty-eight-year-old man who was accustomed to making thousands of dollars a day in the streets. Using the same mind-set, approach, and leadership skills I developed in the streets, I eventually branched off independently and built a $500,000 transportation and logistics company in a little more than a year.

The CEO of one of the companies I'd had a contract with witnessed firsthand how hard I had been hustling to fulfill contracts for his company through my own company, Courier-Logix. When he started having severe chest pains in his sleep, he began to realize that he had no one in place to take over his company or secure his retirement. He called me in for a meeting to share this very concern and we agreed that I would begin to position myself to take over his entire operation.

He and his wife had been running their business for twenty-five years, but they needed new and innovative ideas to help grow and scale. We agreed that I could keep my own company and continue being paid through my company, but if I could double his business portfolio, I would be given 49 percent equity ownership. This placed all of the expectation and responsibility on me without having any assurances of profit-sharing in the new contracts. I was taking a major risk, and, if I allowed it to rule, my street mentality would not have allowed me to place myself in that type of predicament where there are no guarantees. The difference is at this place in my life I was fearless in my faith and therefore we had a deal! He agreed to take me to two national small-business events, where he would introduce me as his successor, and then I would be on my own to prove my ability to earn my seat at the table—a daunting and intimidating task I agreed to. I then generated the million dollars in new business I was challenged with in just six months. I had never been in the rooms where this level of strategy and money was being talked about; I was getting exposure and validation I'd lacked, which fueled me to tap into a gift of business and leadership that I never knew I possessed. I was also inspiring brothers back home by letting them see what I'd accomplished by turning my life around and owning a successful business that was competing on a national level. Over the next two years, the company was still rapidly growing. But it seemed like the more revenue we brought in, the more problems we had.

FANTASIA

This was one of those areas in our marriage where Ken and I realized how much we shared in common. I had this gift but was having to work too hard to make ends meet. Even though I'd made a change in my team once, I still didn't have control over the money; I didn't have control over my account; I didn't know how much was coming in; I didn't know how much was going out. Once again, I found myself in a position where I didn't have as much money as I thought I had.

KENDALL

When we first met, I appeared to be thriving and overachieving and she appeared to be thriving and overachieving. My wife was a monster moneymaker before we married; I was a monster moneymaker before we met. Yes, we hustle, we do dynamic things. We knew we would make a powerful couple.

But once God brought us together and gave us a safe place in the midst of our marriage, the true health and conditions of our businesses began to become visible. And neither of us was prepared for what we would have to face next.

FANTASIA

By the time Kendall and I came together, I had already lost a lot, but God was beginning to bring it all back. And now you know the story of Ken's comeback.

But once we got married, two forces had been brought together; we started watching everything more closely and now we had two sets of spiritual eyes working on our behalf. All of a sudden all this betrayal comes up. I am not an expert in business, but I'm the one who can sense things; I can feel when something's coming. I have a keen sense of discernment. I've developed the ability to see a person's vibe even before I see their paperwork. So when Ken would talk about his business, it was like, "I've seen this before." There was something going on behind his back.

KENDALL

We had already lost things separately. But we started losing things together when we started struggling together. Those first five years were very tough. Everything we stood on—and even the things we outwardly admired about each other businesswise—began to shake. The contracts started to crumble into sand. They were stealing from her; they were stealing from me.

FANTASIA

It was like, "He's pimping me; she's pimping you. She's pimping me; he's pimping you. You're getting pimped over there; I'm getting pimped over here."

We did not come together as a couple to get into business together; that wasn't our desire. We were rocking just fine separately, but over time we discovered that we were getting taken advantage of, being stripped of everything. I knew a little about music, but I did not know how grimy the music industry was. I understood music, but I was still getting more acquainted with the business side. That's when we decided to combine our experience—mine in the industry, and his in business—and start Rock Soul Entertainment.

KENDALL

We decided to jump off the cliff and start our business from scratch. I also decided that I would just offer to buy my partners out in my logistics company and get them out of the way. They told me they would leave immediately if it was a cash deal. Long story short, they rescinded the offer. So, I told them they needed to buy me out; I figured I'd leave with my piece and just keep it moving. At that point, they locked me out of our QuickBooks, the bank accounts, everything. They said they couldn't continue to pay me. During that meeting, they also informed me that they had emptied my office and set boxes full of my belongings outside. After the meeting, I was so upset that I locked myself out of my truck and ended up standing in the parking lot waiting on my wife to come with the spare key. As I sat there, I questioned God. This felt like the moment I first got home from jail, but much worse. I felt violated, powerless, vulnerable, and full of rage. That's when I got so depressed.

FANTASIA

Between Ken's experience and me being pimped, we found ourselves backed into a corner and forced to turn our backs on everybody and trust each other. We went through a time when we walked away from everybody and lost everything. We almost did not have enough money to put on the next show. We could not get our car fixed. We could not work on the house. We didn't have enough money to do the next nothing other than sit at the airport and watch airplanes take off. We had nothing financially, but we had each other.

KENDALL

So, we jumped off the boat of our contracts and onto the shore of our covenant—the place we learned we could trust, a place that offered true loyalty and dependability. From there we could build again. We were clear that we possessed the ability to generate money because we had collectively grossed about $30 million during our first three years of marriage. It is a sexy, inspiring story because we are still standing, but we were under a lot of pressure. We had to overcome some tremendous struggles and setbacks.

Our covenant became the new boat that we took refuge in to go back out into the turbulent sea and face everything that we had to face.

Greater Protection

KENDALL

In marriage, we wrestle with contracts and covenants, and we've learned how important it is to know the proper priority. A covenant is an oath that comes with conditions, a spiritual agreement that is heavenly binding. From a biblical standpoint, it is a promise God makes to human beings about what He will do for them if they do their part in terms of their relationship with Him. For example, God made a covenant with the Israelites that He would protect them if they kept His law and were faithful to him. In 2014, when my wife and I entered our marital covenant, we stood as witnesses stating that we would hold each other accountable to our mutual goal of joined forces. We pledged an oath: "for richer, for poorer; for better for worse; 'til death do us part; so help me, God." I didn't say my vows to my wife. I said them to God while she was present. That means if she is in a bad contract; when her knees are killing her; when she has gestational diabetes; when she has a C-section—I'm going to do what I need to do and step my game up.

A contract is an agreement with the world that requires a certain level of performance in a certain time frame. Both of us came into our marriage having contracts, promises, and agreements that related to our work, the world of business, like most couples do. Mine related to my logistics company; hers related to her work in the music industry.

When commitments are ranked spiritually, a covenant rates higher than any contract. And if you uphold your end of the bargain, it will also offer greater protection. So, the most important thing when you are married is to protect your marital covenant from the interference that will inevitably be caused by your worldly contracts, promises, and agreements. But too many married couples and people in relationships lose sight of their covenants because they focus on their contracts. When someone wants to pay my wife to perform, the production is going to be lit. We're going to make sure everyone's in a great spirit, that the lights are right, that the harmonies are poppin'. When someone pays me to come speak, I'm going to prepare; I'm going to have visuals; I'm going to be on time; I'll make sure my tie is straight. Both of us are going to give you more than you paid for.

Most people go to great lengths to perform in their professional lives. But do you do that for your marital covenant? Do you actually still put the same level of effort into your relationship as you do into your work? Do you get dressed with the same zeal, enthusiasm, ambition, inspiration, and motivation to honor the fine print of your covenant like you do for your contract? Do you still put forth the effort when things are not going the way you would like? Do you go all out, forgive, be patient, love, cuddle, do romantic things even though your mate might not reciprocate or you're not getting the return on that investment you usually do? Do you still give flowers if you can't have sex? Will you still cuddle if the person is not in the mood to talk?

Do you deliver for your covenant what you deliver for your contract? Because you can't serve both God and man. So it's important to ask: Do I put in the same level of performance for my relationship that I do for my career? Do I do it with the same joy?

FANTASIA

We tend to give the world our best. If you're anything like me, you will show up; you will overdeliver. We will wait backstage, so to speak, for as long as it takes to advance our careers. We'll speak to a thousand people even though in the moment we may not quite be up to it. But then in dealing with our mate, there may be moments when we don't call when we are supposed to. We may talk over them or disrespect them. I know that I've done these things; I also know I'm not alone. Why do we sometimes perform on a higher level for our worldly contracts than our covenants?

God is calling us to show more character and be more of a full-grown husband or wife when it comes to our covenant requirements than we are in the world of our contracts.

Your Covenant Is Your Life Raft

KENDALL

The beginning of our relationship gave my wife and me a dramatic example of why it's important to prioritize your covenant over your contracts. Because we were being exploited so badly, we had to jump off the boat of our contracts and onto the shore of our marital covenant almost right away. Even while we were still getting to know each other, we were forced to trust each other and turn our backs on everyone else. Our covenant was a place where we learned to trust, a place that offered true loyalty and dependability. From there we were able to begin building again.

To this day, I thank God that my wife had a gift that somebody couldn't take away from her. They might have been able to play with the money or other things, but they could not take her gift in the same way that they had taken my position at my company. That said, they could not take my wisdom, strategic mind-set, and leadership mastery either. Our gifts and talents, skills and abilities, were the only things we had—and the only things, God showed us, that we needed. She still had the ability to command audiences around the country and around the world. So, I took every single gift, talent, and skill set that I was using in my industry and my business and brought it over to her singing gift—and that lovemaking between gifts birthed Rock Soul Entertainment. Her gift became the life raft for both of our talents, until we were able to reach a new destination and try a different approach.

FANTASIA
God saved us.

KENDALL
Our journey was rocky. We had conversations and understandings and misfires and second-guessing.

FANTASIA
There were moments when we had so much friction that we began to have regrets. Should we have done this? Was this the right thing?

There were times when I wondered, *Do I need to just do my own thing?* We experienced egos, competition, strife, so on and so forth. We had growing pains. It took a lot of circumcising of our egos and selfishness and impatience to get to that place where we could rock with unity, harmony, and agreement.

But we reached a place where it had become clear that we couldn't trust in the contracts no matter what. That's when we discovered that if we continued to trust in each other and trust God, He'd let everything make sense. God started to show us: This is my bag; this is Ken's bag. Here's what I can do that he can't do; and here's what he can do that I can't do. As we continued to trust in God, we learned to trust in each other.

Along the way, we stopped clashing and started finding out how to work parallel to each other and complement each other. By the time we reached the shore of our new destination, we knew exactly who we were. And by learning from those experiences, we could multiply and duplicate things in other ways.

KENDALL

Looking back, we jumped off the cliff into business just like we'd jumped off the cliff into marriage. Both times, we were just starting to understand each other and develop communication by learning each other's strengths, weaknesses, and our pet peeves as a husband and a wife, even though we didn't yet have a rhythm. In business, I didn't know her; she didn't know me. I didn't understand how she approached shows; she didn't understand how I approached balance sheets, profit and loss, cost, and so on. We had to relearn each other—one part marriage, one part business—but now we are learning simultaneously.

We honored our covenant agreement more than our contractual agreements, and God honored His covenant with us. When the contracts tried to destroy us, it was the covenant the world couldn't break. God got us to this place we never could have imagined, coming from such a broken place—where a ministry would be birthed out of a marriage that took place in three weeks and went through such hardship. It's our covenant that also birthed *Taylor Talks* and the very book you now hold in your hands.

Serve Each Other

KENDALL

Because our relationship started out the way it did, even though we faced lots of challenges, our issues were not centered on whose career would come first or what roles each of us would play in our home and family life. To this day, we don't deal with any of that. We believe in serving each other. That is our lifestyle.

At home we don't really see chores as the man's chores or the woman's chores. We divide chores; both of us do everything. We both do whatever needs to be done. Do you see it? Do it. We are a unit. This is what we do. It's too easy to develop friction related to the tick and the tack of life. The only thing we will fall out about is if she touches the trash because I'm not having that. But anything else? I'll fold the clothes. I'll do dishes. I'll do floors. She'll do the bed, get the groceries, cook the dinner. Whatever needs to be done, we just do it.

FANTASIA

When you both do everything, you move off the table things that you might otherwise debate about or lord over the other person. We're both competitors and I'll say, "I got it," and he will say, "No, I got it." We both care so much for each other that we go hard for the other.

I like to do the clothes, but when I was pregnant, I needed all the help I could get, so he had to take that off me. The other night, though, I got the sheets out of the dryer to put on the bed. He grabbed the sheets from the other side, and we put them on. He was as tired as I was, so we did it together. It was like, "Let's get these sheets on the bed so we can both lie down."

We highly recommend that you serve your partner.

KENDALL

In our business life, we each take on what we do naturally. We submit to the other's gifts. So, she takes care of everything creative. I don't worry about her stuff—harmonies, show, stage, dance moves, wardrobe. Don't care; ain't worried about it. I handle everything executive. She doesn't have to worry about anything with the production crew, any kind of hiccups that happen, anything going on logistically, missed flights, price negotiations, this, that, and the third. That's not her concern. Between the two of us, the show goes off without a hitch. We give each other a kiss, a high five after the show is over, and then we get ready to do it again.

FANTASIA

When he speaks, I don't worry about his speech, what he'll say, how he'll say it, what he's going to wear, or how he's going to get there. I'll worry whether once he gets there, are they going to have what he needs? How does his mic sound? What are the theatrics? Does he have quiet time before he goes onstage? Because when you do shows or speaking engagements, people who are part of the show want to talk to you; they want pictures. All of that's fine; they want a piece of the gift. But lots of times people don't know that an artist needs quiet time, so they don't experience "static," where you feel kind of cloudy during the performance. We need time to be silent, to be still so our performance can be on point. I told him about that. Sometimes I may give Ken creative tips. He spoke at one prison where there were some guys on death row, some who had life sentences. They're hard nuts to crack. I've been there, done that with rough crowds before. So, I was like, "Ken, why don't you come out with some music?" He was like, "Yeah, that's really dope!" He did it and killed it.

So, we kind of go back and forth with each other. I don't speak as well as he does. He doesn't sing as well as I do. But we both have something to offer and we do our best to bring forth each other's gifts. Competition will always blind you to the gifts that are present, waiting to help you complement one another. In marriage it truly is us against this world.

Fly and Be Free

FANTASIA

Our covenant means supporting each other's spiritual callings and dreams. For us, that raises the issue of life on the road. Because I've done the road life for so many years, I can tell you it's not anywhere as glamorous as you may think.

KENDALL

A lot of people would see my wife's stage performance, some music videos, and think, *That's the life.* That's how many people picture it, like every day is a music video.

FANTASIA

No, you hop on a bus or plane, you arrive, you unpack, you got an hour. You go to the venue for a sound check. Ken goes to talk to the production team, talk to the tour manager, make sure everything's right.

KENDALL

I'll make sure everything's right on the videos, check to see if the monitor's got everything straight, confirm with Marciano that all the gear is there. Then we go back to the hotel, get something to eat, maybe have two hours, might take a nap if we can sleep. Sometimes I'll head up to the venue while she's backstage and getting prepared.

FANTASIA

You do all of this stuff, then you go onstage for anywhere between forty-five and ninety minutes.

KENDALL

Of course, she knocks the show out.

FANTASIA

Then we eat some cold food that we had to order at 8:00 because you don't get offstage 'til 10:30. Hop on the bus, go to the next city, or catch a 6:00 a.m. flight to come back home and become Mom and Daddy again.

Road life doesn't look like that for every business traveler, but that's what it really looks like for me. So, I am excited about Ken now taking over a little more of it. After two pregnancies where it was just me as the breadwinner—I was the mom and the dad, wearing my Tim boots—I'm ready to chillax a little bit and do the mommy thing. The fact that I have him makes it a lot easier.

I understand that a lot of women are not in my position, not where I sit today. I wasn't always in this position either, so I have both perspectives. The point is that road life isn't easy, so you just have to be supportive of the person who's on the road—or who has the deadline, or who is building their business, or who is going for their dream. Dreams require sacrifice, and in a marriage both people will have goals and aspirations. Sacrifice is required across the board. It begins first at home and then moves out into the marketplace once the foundation of the home is secure. Remember, after the applause of the crowd or office fades away, it's the home that gives you back what you need to be comfortable in your own skin.

I feel like, if you have a gift, I got to support you with it. I don't want to get in trouble with God, whether or not that involves going on the road. Either way, I don't want to be the one saying, "Well, you should be here." So, while you're off doing your thing—even if you're at school taking classes—I'm going to figure out what God has for me. When Ken's gone, that gives me a pinch of quiet time. That gives me a moment to get with God and hear what He's telling me. I play my meditation bowls or get my meditation in, do some yoga. He's doing his thing; I'm doing my thing.

When he comes back from his trips, we have conversations. "How was your day? Tell me what happened. But also, let me tell you what God showed me while you were gone, when I had an extra moment of quiet." And then we go off exploring that direction God's sending us. Sometimes it's just a little easier for me to hear God when we're apart.

But I think that we as a whole—men and women, marriages, couples—we have to take that time and allow the person to fly and be free and do what it is that God is calling them to do.

KENDALL

Even though we live a higher-profile life, these principles apply to everyone.

Whether you're a bus driver, a lawyer, or a school social worker, everybody wants more out of life, and we want more because we've been created for more. There are a lot of people who have great jobs, great benefits, stability, and security, but are still wrestling with that thing, that dream, that's burning inside of them. They're wondering, *Am I living at my full potential?* And we're all gifted and burdened with that same thought. Nobody wants to reach the finish line having not lived life to the fullest.

It's one thing to live. It's a completely different thing to be alive.

So, these ideas we're talking about apply to anybody who is fearful, anybody who has become addicted to complacency but has a burning desire to do something more, especially in a relationship. For some people, that might involve jumping off that cliff and getting married. For some people their dream does not lie in business—everybody's not called to be a leader; everybody's not called to be an entrepreneur. Maybe you are an entrepreneur of your home. You don't need to be a doctor or a lawyer to feel accomplished. Because there are lots of people who you might traditionally call successful, but their children are in and out of jail or twerking on TikTok.

Perhaps you are a blue-collar couple, a middle-class couple raising godly children who are respectful and mannerable, who are going to college. Children who are very clear on their self-identity and self-confidence because, instead of trying to reach for worldly accolades, they've been searching inside for validation as you taught and instructed them.

No matter who you are, it's important to identify your gifts, figure out how you can serve each other, and bring your gifts together in ways that complement each other so you can turn away from the world, examine your life together, and look at what God has given you. How do you steward that to the utmost? How can you give God a return on what He's given you? He may have just given you a child that you never thought you could have, like He's given us. That is wealth that He is asking you to steward and to return an increase. So, He's like, "I'm going to give you this child, but I also want this child to be developed, to be healthy, to be God-fearing and to make an impact out there in the world."

If your child is able to do that, and that seed becomes a tree you can draw fruit from, that's success. Integrity, respect, and honor plant seeds you can glean from: peace, pride, and love. God gives you a child and wants a return on that investment. Fear the Lord, be loving and mannerable, and have a productive impact on the world. That takes planning, strategy, discipline, intentionality, budgeting food, groceries, deals—business isn't always the marketplace. It takes a lot just to run your home. It takes a lot just to balance your finances and lead your own tribe and your own clan. All of these types of things involve growth. They don't have to come from a place of money or greed; just live your life at maximum capacity.

You Run the Rhythm

FANTASIA

Of course, this brings up the covenant associated with raising and caring for our children. My grandmother used to tell me, "To whom much is given, much is required" (and see Luke 12:48). In other words, you've got to put a lot in if you want to get a lot out. Everyone is afraid of that part, but it is what it is. You can get out only what you put in. There's no way around that.

KENDALL

No business deal or job can give me the level of validation I get when I see my contribution to my wife and children. There's no applause that I'm ever going to receive for any speech or any contract that compares.

FANTASIA

You have to sit down and study your family and figure out what each person needs. We have a twenty-five-year-old, a twenty-year-old, a ten-year-old, grandchildren, and now a baby. What does the baby need? What does the oldest need? Every person is different. Every family is very different. Somebody else's family may not require what my family requires.

For women, it's especially important for us to figure out our rhythm as the queen and our covenant with ourselves. There are times when we push ourselves to the back burner because of our kids; that's just something we have to do. But also figure out, What's your rhythm as queen of the house? You run the rhythm. You set it up. They're kids; they're going to follow what you do. Many times, your husband will also follow what you do. "What time are we going to eat, babe?" You have to set your own schedule, while at the same time making sure you don't lose yourself in it.

I see women who are not ready to break generational curses, so they stay in relationships that aren't good for them. I also see women who use relationships and children like a pacifier to comfort themselves about other things they are hurting from and dealing with. Some of us spoil them; they don't have to touch anything. We cook, we clean, we cater to their every need. But when we do that, we're not teaching them or passing down the tools they'll need just in case something happens to us. Next thing we know, we have twenty-, thirty-, forty-year-old kids who don't know how to do anything because they're still our pacifier, and we are still not ready to heal.

To fulfill our covenant with our children, it's important to give them responsibilities and prepare them to be independent. King and I do not let our kids take over our relationship to such an extent that we have no time for each other. We'll talk about that more in chapter 9.

Ken and I have our hiccups. We sit down and talk them out and then we'll erase them. We'll notice that this works or that doesn't work. Sometimes we'll have to come back and remind ourselves that when we do this in our household, that happens. We pay attention to what works and what does not work. What hurts him? What hurts me? What makes him happy? What makes me happy? Then we try to apply that knowledge every day.

KENDALL

Many women will naturally take the lead in the domestic environment, but at the same time it's important for the man to be observant and an active participant. On top of his covenant as a father, it's up to him to forecast and plan for contingencies. To plan for all the resources needed, inventory the supplies, the money, the balancing of time. You can't just sit back and wait while your wife or your partner gets burned out, or just assume that she will cover everything at home. Who's leading?

Most Black fathers are very involved with their children, though some aren't, but lots of men in general need to be more active in the home. That means seeing the demands on her and saying, "Okay, I'm going to come sweep this off your plate." I'm not going to tell my wife, "Well, you always do the dishes, you always mop the floor," when I can see she's overloaded doing something for us. No, let me just come right over there and clean up. There have been days when my wife was burned out and tired from the pregnancy. I wasn't gonna wake her up and say, "Babe, do you want me to get Dallas from school?" She needed to sleep, so I'd just insert myself to bring some relief and maintain the consistency. She would wake up and text me, like, "Where you at?" "I'm picking Dallas up." You ain't got to ask me, I'm there.

FANTASIA

Big ups, King!

KENDALL

As men, it's also important that we not sit back and wait on something to fall just because we haven't been doing it as our chore. Because at the end of the day, if something crashes, it ain't just that your wife forgot, you also allowed it to happen. In that regard, managing a home is no different than managing any other enterprise. At work, if somebody embezzles, or somebody gets a harassment charge, a package comes up missing, an employee is underpaid, or whatever, you can't just lift your hands and be like, "Nah," because you weren't the one who did it. It's the same thing with your household. We men have to be engaged, and we have to participate in the whole environment. This is a way that we can add value.

When we don't add value, what we become is the oldest baby in the house. Now you need your clothes washed and folded. Now you need to be reminded of important family matters and your Pamper changed. You need a bottle of your favorite beer ready but are oblivious to how to serve anyone else. You need to be isolated during your Sunday game time. You need to be swaddled. Nah, you got to be a man at all times and at all costs.

FANTASIA

Most women have their hustle on, but I have the same thoughts about women who want to sit around and have a man take care of them. You can't just sit there letting the man burn himself out. You have to do this together. Today, there are so many stay-at-home moms who also have a business. They're making sure the house is clean, the kids are fed, and the homework is done, but they're also hustling things like headbands, hair products, shoes, and design services. You can do it together and it can become whatever you want it to become. Whatever you apply yourself to, just bring your best to it.

KENDALL

I am of the belief that you are either adding to or subtracting from your home environment; there is no middle ground. Both my wife and I cook when it's needed, but she can really create magic in the kitchen. I also know of wives who don't cook and people who live alone that have never learned the skill set of putting raw ingredients together to produce a meal. This is perfectly fine, but please consider, whether you're a woman or a man, how do you afford to eat out all the time? How does it fit into your budget? Don't get mad when times are hard, and you don't have any "rainy day" money or financial investments. When you eat out all the time, you're eating your kids' scholarship, your savings, and your retirement. I enjoy bringing my wife a dish I've cooked. She'll start swinging her legs and be like, "Ooh-la-la!"

To deal with the socioeconomic dynamic that is shifting in this country, a lot of families might need to adjust roles and responsibilities so that they and their home can survive—so they can be "us against the world" in a world that is definitely working against them.

There are a lot of fellas who'd better wake up. You can't keep looking for your mama; keep being that caveman, searching for a wife who will do the dishes, iron your clothes, and live her life being at your service. Because you know what? She's out there trying to get her master's degree. She's out there climbing the corporate ladder, dealing with male chauvinism, and battling your male counterparts. She needs you not to be insecure and add further stress. Your strength as the man in your home fuels the confidence she needs to effectively face men outside of your home.

Learn to take care of yourself, so you don't need to stay with somebody just because they treat you like a baby, or like your mother did. There's no need to be in a situation that's not healthy for you just because she takes care of you. When you can take care of yourself as a man, you can be more selective about finding the woman that God wants for you.

But when you come home asking her to dim her light to do these mundane things that you could be doing and contributing to, you're not just hurting her, you're actually holding your bloodline back. You could be working collaboratively to go out there and do something on a higher level. Let's get the laundry and the cleaning out of the way so you can move your bloodline forward by focusing on greater and more significant challenges that actually add value.

FANTASIA

And many of us come from people who couldn't raise their own kids because they were raising somebody else's. People who had to work out in the field. Now we can come together to do our own thing for our bloodline. Let's kill it!

THE TAYLORS

We are living in different times than we grew up in. Today it's harder to honor your covenants over your contracts, but God will reward you when you do. Trust God and if it's God's will, it will happen. We don't want you to get distracted by your contracts with the world when you have God-given gifts, and He has a calling for you. So, we want you to pull out your journal and reflect upon these questions about what God has for you:

- What spiritual or godly covenants are in place in your life? What covenants do you want to activate to help you be the person God created you to be, the partner God created you to be, the parent God created you to be, and to position yourself for your next season?
- If you could be 100 percent confident that you would be covered financially, and if you weren't afraid you'd fail or

embarrass yourself, and your haters suddenly transformed into your elevators, and you could be 100 percent guaranteed that you'd succeed, what do you see in your dreams and envision in your mind's eye for yourself, your relationship or marriage, and your family? What do you think God wants you to do with your life and your mate and your family?

- Sometimes we need to ask ourselves questions such as: How can I build my confidence? How can I build my self-esteem? How can I triple my net worth? How can I expand my network? Or whatever foundational questions you need to ask so you can grow as individuals, as a couple, and as a family. Ask them and answer them. Don't get frustrated or down on yourself if you don't know all the answers. Just write what you know. God's call on your life will unfold bit by bit over time; you can never see all of it.

CHAPTER 8

MIXED INGREDIENTS
Smoothing Out Your Blended Family

FANTASIA

When a group of singers submit their voices to their choir director, producer, or even one another, they start to harmonize, blend,
and smooth out their rough edges and create something greater than
any of them could have accomplished on their own. Case in point, if
you're much younger than we are, there's a song I want to introduce
you to: "We Are the World." The song was a fund-raiser produced
back in 1985 by the supergroup U.S.A. for Africa. If you've never
heard it before, I want you just to go on YouTube and search it. The
song was created to raise money to help people suffering during a
famine.

Quincy Jones was the song's producer. If you don't know about him, I want you to learn about him too. He's one of the Greats! He started as a musician back in the 1950s. In those days, he played the trumpet for these big jazz groups like Dizzy Gillespie's band—your grandparents or great-grandparents probably used to listen to them. He also started arranging jazz groups and conducting them. Then he went on to become a composer, arranger, record producer, and a producer for movies and TV shows. So, Quincy had double for his trouble.

Q, as many people call him—was born in 1933, so if I ever meet him, I will call him Mr. Jones—produced Michael Jackson's *Off the Wall* and *Thriller* albums and worked with a bunch of other artists. Another of his many gifts is he can hear the next big hit before it happens, but then also go into the office and arrange all the contracts. He is a smart whiz! My King is kind of like him.

More than fifty different singers and musicians performed "We Are the World."[1] Only someone who was a genius like Quincy Jones could take so many different singers and make a beautiful song with them. He had Diana Ross, Michael Jackson, Cyndi Lauper, Whitney, Stevie, Lionel Richie, Tina Turner, Ray Charles, Bruce Springsteen, Luther, Bono; and even more greats. Everybody. I mean he had every major vocalist. To me, it is amazing how he was able to take some of the biggest, highest-paid singers in the world and put them all together in a recording studio, all in one room. They learned the song together and committed and submitted to the project. Some people sang a few lines of their own, but nobody had a long solo. Sonically he chose all the right notes, and sounds, and instruments that pulled you, so that still to this day, when you turn it on, you want to hear

---

1. Wikipedia, s.v. "We Are the World," last modified September 1, 2021, https://en.wikipedia.org/wiki/We_Are_the_World#USA_for_Africa_musicians.

more. It still blows everybody's mind that he had the greatest in one room all singing the same song.

KENDALL

Everybody surrendered all of their gifts and their egos to a higher message and a higher purpose, and they created something that is timeless and has never since been duplicated in that same capacity or with that level of impact.

FANTASIA

At the end of the week, Quincy was probably in heaven—to walk out with such a dope song after just seven days! But that's a lot of different personalities to work with. They probably got stories for days, 'cause, you know, artists can be a bit much. Q probably was like, "Deal with every personality; give 'em what they want; ignore it; get 'em here." I'm sure it was a lot to handle, but look at the outcome. By coming together, submitting, and blending as a group under Quincy's leadership, they created a classic song that almost forty years later is still the eighth-highest-selling song of all time.

But you've got to have that one Quincy Jones–type person who can put you in the room to show you that it actually does work when you submit to one another. Together they raised $63 million for a great cause—saving lives. That's the equivalent of $147 million today. By blending the artists' voices, gifts, and fans, Quincy Jones and "We Are the World" made magic and a big impact. And that's how I think about the power of us blending our families. For Kendall and me, God is our Quincy Jones, 'cause He said, "Okay, I'm gonna put you and your children together and I'm gonna make your relationship work."

Redeeming the Moment

KENDALL

Blending a family is no joke! Every member has different needs, personalities, backgrounds, and gifts, and your children might be at different stages of development. They may still be hoping for your previous relationship to get back together. They may not have completely bought into your new spouse or their new stepsiblings. Still, a new family is being formed, and you need to coparent effectively with their other parents without undermining them. As parents you form the root of the new family tree you're creating. The challenges of adding new members is like carefully selecting the right plants that can coexist in the same garden.

FANTASIA

I came into our relationship with Dallas, who was a toddler then but who's ten as I write this book, and Zion, who was thirteen then and is nineteen now.

KENDALL

I have a son, Treyshaun, who was in his late teens then but is twenty-five now. He has two children and is married. My grandsons are older than Keziah, my daughter with my wife.

My relationship with Trey has had seasons of complication. When I had him at fifteen, I was a kid still looking for his missing father but now having to be a father. I had no identity; I had no foundation. I would get shaken by anything coming my way. There's a lot more to the story about why my life took the turn it did, but putting all that aside, the bottom line is, I got caught up in the dope game for about twelve years. Years of running the streets stole very key moments away from me and Trey that can never be recaptured. Before God's loving conviction, I was on a path of repeating the same cycle I experienced with an absent father. The only difference was that my father was addicted to using drugs, and I was addicted to selling them. I didn't want to leave Trey without feeling a father's love. I wanted to give him a sense of identity, make sure he did well in school, protect him from bullying, help him develop a work ethic, talk about girls, teach him life lessons, and give him those kinds of father-and-son things that I hadn't received. My time of being an occasional and spotty dad had come to an end and now I went after my son with a vengeance. But by then he was already twelve and so much had happened, and my relationship with his mother came with all the complications you would expect.

When I started turning my life around, there was a point where I had a nighttime delivery route. I could finish it by 10:00 or 11:00 p.m., but it didn't have to be done until 2:00 a.m. My route went through Gastonia, where my son still lived. He played football and basketball. So I would stop in my work clothes, park, watch his whole game, and greet him real quick and tell him I loved him. Then I'd hop back on my route. It added about another three hours to my night, but it was a way that I could be there for my son. I didn't miss a game 'cause I was working, because I had the luxury of my route running through his city. And though the process was bumpy and didn't always go the way I planned, over time, Trey and I have both worked and fought to build and protect the bond that we share and cherish today.

I don't have a time machine so I can go back and fix what I never had from my father. I can't fix what I didn't do when Trey was a child. But what I can do is build upon what we have now and enjoy it. What we can do together is redeem this moment. That is the cure. So, for me it has become important to make sure Trey knows that unlike the streets and my years of immaturity, our new blended family is not a threat and will never replace the bond we fought so hard to rebuild and re-create.

FANTASIA

Even though I had Zion so young and spent so much time performing on the road, emotionally I was always there for her. But I had her when I was very young and I was forced to raise her as a single mother. I love my daughter, but I wish I could have had her at an age where I possessed the maturity that I have today. I also wish I had listened to my mother and grandmother, who had already been there, done that. When I was a teenager, they were telling me, "Slow down; slow your roll; take your time; just don't put it all out there." I thought I was so in love; I thought I knew what love was. Man, I'm still figuring out this love thing and I'm thirty-six years old. But at least now I can help another young person by sharing my story.

For years, it was just Zion and me, until Dallas came along. Then I met Kendall. I had to get that rhythm right. The relationship attached to Dallas's arrival was toxic, and Zion was like, "I don't like this song; it was just me and you." So I had to make some changes to create a more harmonious rhythm. In my mind, I think of my job as a mother in a blended family as being like Quincy Jones or the choir director who's always listening to all the different voices and trying to lead them to create the best sonic combination. In our family we just gotta figure out that somebody sitting in the soprano section might excel better as an alto, and who is singing a note that don't sit quite right. Even in music, blending's not always easy.

KENDALL

We were naive when we got married but we weren't foolish. It usually takes members of a blended family several years to bond and become tight with each other. I knew I needed to build a relationship with Zion and Dallas; I wanted my wife to build a relationship with Trey. We wanted our children to build relationships with one another.

With Zion, she always had to share her mom with the world, so building my relationship with her took time. She needed to know that I cared for her and loved her apart from her mother, just as Trey and my wife have to build an island of understanding apart from me. Dallas is with us every other week, so we adjust and recalibrate his needs biweekly. But all of this takes careful handling and understanding to keep the family circle intact. We are blessed that the arrival of Keziah has brought everything closer and full circle. Something about her fight to come home from the NICU and her spirit became the glue that was needed to seal our hearts into one.

FANTASIA

When you're blending your family, it's important to set realistic expectations. Blended families do not "restore the years the locusts have eaten" (see Joel 2:25), and cannot turn back time to re-create whatever your family might have looked like in the past. You have to give everybody room, have realistic expectations, and give everyone time to find their notes and blend. The different people in the family may not find their notes quite as fast as you hope, especially when teenagers are involved. But be patient so, over time, you can create an atmosphere where everyone can grow and develop.

Family activities have helped us build our relationships. Try creating shared experiences. Think: movie nights, day trips, family vacations and rituals such as making homemade pizzas from scratch—to help your blended family bond.[2]

---

2. Jeanne Segal and Lawrence Robinson, "Blended Family and Step-Parenting Tips," HelpGuide, https://www.helpguide.org/articles/parenting-family/step-parenting -blended-families.htm.

KENDALL

The roots in this family tree come from my wife and myself. We have to keep everyone connected and be mindful of who we are to one another. It's been really important for us to parent together, not separately. When it comes to blended families, discipline can be a very sensitive topic, especially when your kids are teenagers.

FANTASIA

From the beginning, you have to identify what discipline is going to look like, and then adjust in whatever ways make sense as your relationships grow and your children develop. A new stepparent shouldn't be the Enforcer in the beginning. No, work with your partner to set the boundaries and limits that help your kiddos feel safe and know that you love them. And speak life into their spirits so they feel valued, loved, and secure.

KENDALL

At times parenting can feel like the roots of most plants, which live beneath the surface; you don't always get recognized for the sacrifices and contributions that you supply to the branches and leaves. Still, you must build your relationships, engage with your children thoughtfully, and always remain in position for the tree to grow and flourish.

I came into this marriage with a strategy in mind. I would devote myself to learning how to best connect with Zion and Dallas and learn how they were emotionally designed and wired personality-wise. Once I understood them for who they truly were, I then knew I could love them in the manner they both needed from me as a father figure. Once that love, trust, and authenticity had been rooted, the only discipline that would ever be required from me would be my disappointment. I have put intentional effort and work into earning the love and respect of both Zion and Dallas to where my opinion and pride in them are the things they most desire. Love became the only leverage needed to create order as the head of this family. I have loved them directly in such a customized way that my love in itself has become the disciplinary rod that I've rarely ever had to wield. No belt or punishment could have more impact than my displeasure in a particular conduct or decision made. While in some cases, physical discipline may be required in certain homes, it can never have more impact than emotional discipline when seeds of love have taken root in fertile soils of innocence.

It is key to gain an understanding of what each child's individual vibrations are. What works for Trey doesn't work for Dallas. What works for Zion may not be effective with Keziah. Knowing how to connect and engage with each child in their own unique way is the beginning of a blended family. Next, we have to determine the overall direction for our family and how to lead each unique personality in that direction. Example, Trey is a grown man who is now married, successful, and can add more value to the family than he needs to withdraw. He is finding fulfillment in being able to give back to the family circle as a leader now himself. Dallas needs constant direction and focus because his mind and belief systems are being crystallized now at the age of ten. His next few years leading up to adolescence are going to be the cornerstone to the next twenty-plus years of his life. Still, both need to feel valued, loved, instrumental to the family, and cherished. The manner in which we show our love and appreciation for them also must come in different forms even though the message itself is very much the same.

FANTASIA

As I look back on my life and relationships, I've learned that we need to be careful with our breaking up and our linking up. Because when you break up, the energy of all that attaches to your children. They ask questions like, Why is my mother over here? Why is my father over there? Same thing when we link up again.

Even though my parents were together for twenty-seven years, I believe their breakup affected our family, especially my younger brother. That's not to say that just because your parents are together, you'll come out fine. I was raised in a family where the mother and daddy were there and in some ways we all have a little bit of crazy.

All of us have a story—we really do. And I can't say that because families are broken up that all kids go through the same thing, because I've seen families that break up, yet the kids come out fine. I've also seen families that are together, but the kids struggle. Kendall grew up with a mother who was present but a father who was absent. He went through some things but look at him now!

KENDALL

We each have to be sensitive about the dynamics in each other's families. My wife's situation with Dallas's dad and stepmom is different from my situation with Trey and his mom, who at this point is grown and has a family of his own. The dynamic of each of our children requires unique and tailored attention in order to maintain. A blended family is not a one-size-fits-all, especially when the children are all different ages.

FANTASIA

Like how Ken teaches me to approach every challenge like a game of chess. You have to figure out what each piece's strengths are, where you need them to be, and which strategy will secure the win!

If you still have your mother and father, speak to them and ask them for advice. Ask, "Mom, what was I like raising a daughter, and how did it compare to raising sons?"

No matter what sacrifices have to be made, it's all really worth it. I notice and watch Dallas. When he sees Kendall and me behaving in a loving way—like when Ken is massaging my feet—something about that makes him happy. He runs in and out of the room.

Sometimes he'll ask, "Y'all call me?"

"Boy, you know nobody called you," we say and laugh.

But he's really, really happy. He's got a smile on his face. He sleeps better at night. He comes alive. As long as you take it a step at a time, kids like to see their parents demonstrate affection.[3] It's like when you put on a good love song and that energy flows through the house like music and sound waves flow through your ears and make you happy.

Moving Together in Rhythm

FANTASIA

It's important to stay connected to your partner. Whatever you do, don't let the kids pull apart your relationship. Check in with each other every day and engage in activities that bring you together— whether that's going fishing or going to the theater to watch the new summer blockbuster. The Bible tells us that love not only perseveres, but love is patient, kind, humble, slow to anger, forgiving, protective, and trusting. Read 1 Corinthians 13:4–8 from time to time to remind yourself. Take the Word to heart.

Don't give up even when times are tough. Every relationship experiences challenges, no matter how perfect things appear to be on social media. Blending a family is no joke, so always remember what brought you together in the first place. If you're going through a rough time, that is to be expected, so it's okay to just admit it. Also, encourage yourselves with some positive affirmations: "At the

---

3. Segal and Robinson, "Blended Family and Step-Parenting Tips."

moment we're going up the rough side of the mountain, but we have faith that we will reach the top and get to the other side."

KENDALL

Being older and more mature, my wife and I wanted to experience having a child together and raising it differently from how we had parented in the past. We wanted this from the time we got married, but I couldn't even conceive of us conceiving until after we figured out how the two of us, my son, and her two children were going to operate as a family. If that wasn't enough, we had all those financial challenges early in the marriage, when we jumped off the cliff and started our own business from scratch. As a man, I didn't want to bring a new child into that situation.

Sometimes I'm too strategic and I can't enjoy the moment because I'm always counting and measuring. I have spent a lot of time thinking of how every time you add a life, you gotta slice the pie differently. Though a lot of people are like, "I love a big family." Everyone wants to have a big Thanksgiving; everyone wants to have that Christmas moment when we all are wearing onesies and our stockings are hanging up on the mantel. But I'm like, "Yeah, but the more people you got, you gotta slice the pie smaller. You gotta slice the time pie; you gotta slice the relationship pie; you gotta slice the financial pie. That's a lot of Pampers and underwear; that's a lot of food; that's a lot of bikes and toys; that's a lot of health care; that's a lot of education. A big budget means big responsibility on your shoulders." This way of thinking has protected me during certain seasons, but it has also blinded me to some of the blessings of life that don't fit into my philosophies as well. There are many large families that may have financial challenges, yet the love, joy, and loyalty remain connected through that very same commonality of suffering. There are families that are small and financially free in some respects, but still there remains turmoil and trauma that's hidden behind name brands and other luxurious coverings. We are imperfect as parents and our family has its imperfections. And this is the very reason why we are perfect for one another.

FANTASIA

Then so much time had passed since we married, I was like, "It took me a long time to get my body to this place and I'm keeping it here. Nah, let's travel instead of having a baby." That's when my mother told me, "You'll be disappointed if you don't have a love child with your husband." I was already in my thirties. I thought about it and realized she was right. But then we found out that my tube was closed. That was a whole 'nother journey. Then we just decided to surrender and let God handle it. Now here we are, with Keziah!

KENDALL

We're trying to find our way. We can't assume that the way my life was with Trey, or the way hers was with Dallas and Zion, is going to be how our life is with all of them plus Keziah. This is a new experience. And everyone now gets a smaller slice of the family pie. However, we're married; we're older; we're in different places in our lives, in our careers, and in our marriage. So we can take advantage of some old principles and things that worked well, though there's also a lot we need to learn that's new.

FANTASIA

As I've said, until Keziah, I never had anyone by my side while I was pregnant before.

KENDALL

And I'd never stood beside somebody who was pregnant with my child. We hope we can break our generational curses and create completely different dynamics for Keziah. It is a beautiful thing because we're in agreement.

That said, our older children might be thinking, *Now you've found love; you have a partner; there are more children; and now there's this baby?* They might not say these things to us, but we know even if they're not thinking it consciously, subconsciously the thought's probably there, setting off alarms. We have to stay aware of that.

FANTASIA

At this point, we've been together for almost seven years. Our family has really begun to blend. We have all made sacrifices and adjustments for the sake of the family circle. Even though we are at different places, ages, and perspectives and have different dreams in life, we remain determined to protect our family's potential by loving with an unconditional heart.

We're working hard, getting better and making progress with our blended-family song, but I guess you could say that we're still in rehearsals. I'm very proud of how far we've come, and though we are still working on our choreography of understanding, whenever we share the stage together, it's a magical moment. If Quincy Jones could produce "We Are the World" with so many of the biggest names in the business, with all those attitudes and egos, we can do the same thing in our family—and we will.

It's not so different from what I know about singing. Performing as a solo artist, I've been singing soprano most of my life and that is my comfort zone on stage, but when it comes to family, I am willing to adjust to a more alto approach because, as Dallas likes to say to me at times, I can be dramatic. And if I am too loud about matters, Zion may go completely silent. To me, marriage and blended family are similar to this. We're a group. The group is so important that I'm willing to try something different. I'll give up singing solo and soprano to sing alto because we're making music collectively and I love it.

As a family, we're still getting it together. We're still figuring out who fits where; who's gonna lead next week; who's gonna fall back. But we know it's gonna end up being a beautiful song.

THE TAYLORS

Now that you're thinking about blending your family, here are some questions to journal, think about, and discuss with each other:

- Ask your partner what values she or he thinks are most important for their children and why, then share what values are most important for your kids and why. Look at the areas of overlap, and come up with a joint list of values that you will talk about with all of your young folks.
- Create a list of routines you want to implement as a family. Ask your children for input, especially your teens.
- Talk to your partner about common discipline problems that could arise and the strategies you will use.
- Consider holding a family meeting to collectively come up with household guidelines, values, and rules.
- Create a family vision and mission plan with your partner. What is God's purpose for your family? What are each family member's gifts, talents, goals, and dreams? What do you want your relationship and household to feel like? What behaviors can you engage in to turn your family into a nurturing and loving place where it feels like Christmas music

is playing all the time? Now write down your family mission and a list of agreements about how you, as a couple, are going to operate.

- Develop a plan that will help you deepen your relationships by first making a list of all your family members and the activities they love to engage in individually. Then use this list to think of activities that will help build relationships with your partner's children. Next, what activities can you plan as a family that tap into common areas of interest? Put them on the calendar as part of your family schedule.

CHAPTER 9

KEEP IT SPICY
Dating for Life

FANTASIA

I pulled out my phone and wrote my husband a text: "What are you doing in an hour?" I asked, even though I'd already scoped out his calendar.

"Working on Salute First, Queen, why do you ask?" he texted back.

"Meet me at our favorite hotel. Room 1229."

"You don't have to ask me twice!"

I put a bottle of his favorite champagne in the ice bucket and set out two champagne flutes, then I pulled out my speakers and started playing some neo-soul to set the mood. I pulled the comforter back and propped the pillows up. Then I pulled a dozen red roses out of their plastic sleeve. I plucked the petals off and carefully sprinkled the rose petals on the floor from the door, to the bed, to the bathroom.

They stood out so beautifully on the white sheets. I put another dozen in a vase that I set on the dresser.

My Ken Doll loves chocolate, so I put white chocolate–coated strawberries on his night table so I could feed them to him. Then I put a handful of Hershey's Kisses on his pillow. The silver foil set off the red roses.

Only ten more minutes more 'til my Ken Doll would arrive. He always arrives on time for our little getaways.

"Text me when you get to the lobby."

"I'm already in the parking lot waiting."

I replied with something spicy that I'll let you imagine. Needless to say, this would be our time—no kids, no managers, no industry executives, no musicians, no parent-teacher conferences, no yards to mow, no floors to sweep or mop. We're all about it!

So many couples are working so hard, and a lot of times when women get pregnant or start having kids, we forget about ourselves; we don't focus on ourselves anymore; it's just about the kids kids kids kids kids. So a few years ago, Ken and I came to an agreement that we need our time. On school nights we cannot wait until everybody in the house goes to bed. That does not work because by the end of the night, the kids are going to wear you out, and sometimes you got that one child who likes to get up and creep. By the time we hit the sack, we would be tired, so we came to an agreement: We've got to switch up the hours. We have to figure out a schedule. We have to figure out how to keep the love and romance alive!

KENDALL

Sometimes we just leave the house and go. Get a hotel room right around the corner so we can have some time to ourselves. And during those times when this isn't possible, we can always sneak away to one of our favorite food spots for a nice meal and glass of wine.

FANTASIA

We protect our dating life so that we continue to revist that feeling of when we first met. We take the little speaker to the hotel and just dance, be romantic, just have a good time. Go to one of our favorite spots, have a staycation. I am very big on doing things he likes, keeping things exciting, keeping it spicy. Do whatever it takes to protect and salvage that area of your life. Because as a woman, if you put all your energy into your kids, the man starts to feel neglected and he's like, "Well, what about me?"

And when I got pregnant, I would send him messages like, "Hey, give me a couple of months; your girl will be back. I'm gonna be a dope mom; I'ma take care of the baby; we'll find a sitter, and I'm gonna give you your time and give Mommy her time as well."

KENDALL

In a sense, a marriage can be like owning a Bentley or a Rolls-Royce. Everybody wants that look. They wanna be in it, they wanna feel successful, they want other people to view them as successful on IG, Facebook; they want to be "hashtag goals," but just because you can afford to get something doesn't mean that you have the means to keep it up.

Looking beyond the wedding, many couples may not have considered the upkeep and the maintenance required to keep a marriage or a relationship up and running. When the communication breaks down on the side of the road, or the sacrifice won't start, or the submission goes out, the insecurities have to go into the shop, and here comes the bill. That's when many people realize that when they owned a Camry, that oil change used to be $80, $90, $120. But the oil change on a Bentley is $600, $800; that repair that used to cost $1,200 is now costing $5,000. Suddenly, they don't want the responsibility; they don't want to make the sacrifice of increasing their income or tightening their belt. Too many of us seem to want a facade that projects something that's not really there. Romance is a part of a marriage's preventive maintenance and even that takes effort.

Kissed, Hugged, and Touched

KENDALL

People often think of romance in a relationship as a feeling of mystery, excitement, and distance from everyday life. But it takes a lot of work to keep those feelings alive in a society that has severely watered down and even rejected the idea of romance and replaced it with lustful substitutions. These days, many people engage in hookups and one-night stands that offer greater risks of catching a sexually transmitted disease rather than the opportunity to achieve any form of lasting satisfaction or emotional closeness. Our twerking pandemic diverts the eyes and hearts of many men and entices them to throw one-dollar bills at strangers instead of taking the time to choose a perfect bouquet of flowers for a woman who challenges their character vs. their currency. And some couples even entertain swinging in an attempt to compound their lack of pleasure that is secretly hidden in feelings of inadequacy. Romantics are almost an endangered species.

We often wonder why the feeling of mystery and excitement has slowly decayed in so many relationships. Is it because we have become too comfortable in our regularity and consistency? Are we afraid to break up our norm because the monotony also gives us a sense of control? Have we given over all of our free time and creative energy to work and children, forgetting that our hustle is supposed to help fund our happiness, and that children are living reminders of what romance can create when we invest quality time in each other? Or perhaps, we allow insecurity to talk us out of trying something new because we fear rejection if our partner is unwilling to participate? Sandwiched between stacked schedules and never-ending commitments, has dating lost its divine power, leaving no room for organic intimacy and connection?

Dating can be a vehicle that keeps lovers moving toward soulmate success. It is a power source that allows two lovers to disconnect from the mundane, the stressful, the frustrating, and even the unsuccessful areas in life. Isn't distance from everyday life one of the most important reasons why we date in the first place? Our relationship is one place where we should always feel wanted, understood, accepted, needed, valued, and victorious.

FANTASIA

Dating is also very important because women are different from men. The way I look at it, most women are pretty emotional. We like to be told that we are beautiful. We like our partner to tell us that he loves us. We like to be kissed, hugged, touched, and to get flowers. Especially when a woman has children, she is cooking, and she is cleaning; it is important to her to feel special. I love that kind of stuff. It also lets me know that I am doing things okay. He is good; he is satisfied. If Ken goes a day or two without reassuring me, I am like, "Are you okay? Are we okay?" But to be honest, he never goes a single day without telling me just how beautiful I am in his eyes.

KENDALL

Normally, as soon as she wakes up, I tell my wife how beautiful she is. That way she hears it from me before she talks to anyone else. I give her a kiss and say good morning. As a man, I did not realize until this marriage how important romance is to me also. There is a silent competition that I have with myself. It is the way I gauge if I am a successful husband or not. Because as important as they are to my Queen, words are fleeting. Happiness can come and go. I am always looking to do things that keep her full of butterflies, give her something to look forward to, keep something new on her calendar, and shake things up.

I have realized that romance is an investment that pays great dividends. It is a lot like a stock. You invest in a stock; you are looking for a financial return. I realize that if I keep her cup full, she is going to make sure I am overflowing. Her happiness has become my strength. It seems cliché, but truth be told, when she is happy, I can focus; I can grind. I know I have her support. I know I am covered. That is very important to me, and that comes from taking time out for romance.

FANTASIA

Every now and then, he will text me from the office things like, "Your happiness and seeing you smile makes me have all of these ideas." I think that plays a part for both of us. If we are not communicating well and we are upset, neither of us can do anything, real talk. Ken cannot write. It throws us off. We are not just saying that.

KENDALL

A year after we got married at the courthouse, we had a wedding in real life on a yacht in Charlotte. We had our ceremony and partied all night on the water with our mothers and aunties, about seventy-five guests, a full band, and this guy Fantasia sang "Georgia" with earlier when he had been playing the keyboard on the dock. He joined us when the boat came back to the dock later on and sang and played with us. The celebration was so joyful that people didn't want to get off the boat. In fact, we partied for so long that they cut the lights out on us. It may sound corny, but there was that moment when she was coming down the aisle. Seeing her in her dress, boohooing and stating her vows, I was blown away. Reaffirming my commitment to her as part of our covenant, as her partner, was one of the most romantic moments of my life.

FANTASIA

There was another time that is one of my most romantic memories. I came home one day and I saw both my kids just chilled out lying with Ken, both really quiet. Dallas is a Sagittarius, Zion is a Leo, and they do not always follow when it comes to Mommy. So when I walked into the room, I saw everybody gathered, and Trey was living with us too. Everybody was just chilling, and I was like, "Okay, God." That was very romantic to me.

So, a romantic moment can take place at any time, and it doesn't have to be expensive. You can create one with something as simple as a smile or a compliment. But why not make a little effort? Try cooking a hot meal from scratch instead of heating up a frozen one or ordering takeout; or filling the tub with a hot bubble bath that contains milk, essential oils, Epsom salts, and flower petals floating on top; or turning off the lights and lighting candles for dinner, in the bedroom or around the house; or just feeding each other fruit. Try catering to each other or giving each other a massage with a good-smelling oil or treating each other to a spa day.

Power Up

KENDALL

Fantasia and I are big fans of date nights as well, and we think that you can benefit from them too. We are running our business; we are investing in the kids; we've got activities with friends and in-laws; and time was and will continue to be a scarce resource in our lives. But my wife can give me energy that nobody else can give me, and I pray that I have an energy source to give her something that nothing else in this world can give her. Date night is a way for us to disconnect from all that and give each other exactly what we need so that we can power up and get back out there and face the world again.

FANTASIA

I think it's really important to make time for date nights. From the time we got married, I have been very spontaneous. I could just look at Ken and be like, "Let's go to Jamaica." He would be like, "When??" I would be like, "Tomorrow." Then, of course, he would be like, "Okay, but we need to set a budget?"

But I would get the tickets and we would go, and next thing you know, we'd be sitting in beach chairs by a bright blue pool, or on a sandy beach, or snorkeling with all those cute little pretty fish, with the sun beaming down on us, sipping piña coladas, or with the juice from a fresh pineapple or mango dripping down our chins. And then there'd be a dinner of steak and lobster on a cliff overlooking the turquoise blue sea, feeling the trade winds blow my sundress, while steel pan drums played in the background.

But sometimes we get busy and have no time for a date. When we haven't been out or on a date night in a while, I will tell Ken, "All we do is work. I am bored. Baby, we cannot lose our spice."

KENDALL

Many people love to have the chance to get dressed up and go out. I know my wife wants to dress up, put on a nice heel, and show me what I am risking if I play out here in these streets.

We especially love to go out to eat. We have our favorite restaurants, but we also try new restaurants. From time to time, I tell my wife to pack a bag. I have mapped out the spot; I got the reservation; I got the bottle of wine; I went to Victoria's Secret and got her a little pink bag.

I like that feeling. For me, that is success, when I can surprise her and she is like, "What? Where are you taking me?"

"Do not ask me," I tell her. "Just pack a bag."

FANTASIA

When my husband tells me to pack my bags, I get on the phone and say, "Girl, my husband is taking me someplace special! I'm so excited."

KENDALL

Sometimes we explore another city, which can give us a nice change of pace. I also remember the first time I told her I wanted to take her to the mountains. She was like, "Go to the mountains?" I was like, "Yeah, trust me, it will be different." We went and she fell in love with it.

FANTASIA

The view was dope. Before that, I hated rainy days, probably because they reminded me of when I was in a bad place. But up in the mountains, the rain was beautiful; I just listened to the birds. We totally disconnected. Now I love a good rainy day.

KENDALL

My wife likes water, palm trees, Jamaica. Before my relationship with her, I had never been exposed to the islands outside of a cruise where you have a few hours to enjoy the culture while constantly making sure you don't get left at the dock when the ship disembarks. Now St. Lucia is one of our favorite spots to rekindle our romance. Sometimes she'll get booked for a show abroad and we may go three days early or stay two or three days after and turn it into a mini vacation. Sometimes we just go to the beach here in North Carolina.

We'll rent a home with a little pool in the back so we can have some privacy.

FANTASIA

We have had some good times. But I think some of my favorite dates were during the days when we were broke. I'm a Southern, country girl. I'm not into a lot of that celebrity stuff. I drive my own car; I shop for my own groceries; I cook my own food; I do my own laundry; I clean my own house. Ken and I both appreciate and protect the simplicity of things. You don't need a lot of money to enjoy a romantic moment.

Ken knows that I love water. Once during our broke days, he got a cute little boat and we went out on the lake. We were just out there having red wine and listening to music on our little JBL speaker with the blue sky and puffy white clouds floating overhead. I was like, "My husband is gangsta to put something together like this for me." It was just a little boat—so little that I didn't know if we were sinking or swimming. Every time one of those big luxury boats would come by, it would create a big wave. I would be like, "Ken, are we good?" But he was so confident.

The size of our boat did not make us. We would wave our hands at the big boats. They didn't have any idea who was on our little tink-tink of a boat. You see what I'm sayin'? But I fell in love with it and we stayed out there from sunup to sundown.

KENDALL

One of my most fun times was spent on vacation just hopping in one of those little golf carts and riding around town. People were like, "Is that Fantasia in a golf cart?" We would get us some drinks, or ride down to the beach, or ride down to a little food spot. We really have a lot of fun.

10 FUN DATES ON A MODEST BUDGET

On a budget? We feel you. Here are some of our favorite inexpensive dates with a twist:

1. Throw some grape juice or bubbly in a bag with some crackers and cheese. Take them to the park with your blanket or eat them in your car along a lake or river at sunset.
2. Drive-in theaters are making a comeback. Pop some popcorn at home, then go see your favorite flick. For even more fun, you can turn it into a double date!
3. Take salsa or ballroom dance lessons together at your local community center.
4. Identify a cause you both care about, then volunteer together at your church, a senior center, a homeless shelter, or at a local school or nonprofit whose work you support.
5. Go to karaoke night and make fools of yourselves together.
6. Make a mood playlist together and stroll back down memory lane.
7. Go to the bookstore or library and check out a book, then read to each other in a cozy atmosphere.
8. Grab a bottle of wine and a blanket and stargaze.
9. Pull out your pictures from childhood and tell your partner the story of your life.
10. Go bowling, miniature golfing, canoeing, or riding scooters together.

A Lifetime Protection Plan

FANTASIA

One time we were watching a show where all these sisters were gathered around a woman trying on a wedding dress.

The bride said, "Ever since I was a little kid, I always imagined myself at my wedding."

That made me think of how even though I played with Barbies and fantasized about my Ken doll when I was a child, I never had those thoughts about getting married, even as an adult. I didn't see a lot of relationships working out or know of many people my age who had tied the knot. I honestly thought I would be singing "Free Yourself" all my life right up until the time that Ken Doll and I met. But I did think about what I wanted real love to look like if it ever happened to me. I would observe people's relationships when I was young. I could see the marriages that were torn and the marriages that were strong. I saw the wrong and, for some reason, also knew what was right. As I looked at some women, I would think, *If you could just add this, and if the woman could have her kids, but not let herself go, or not get so caught up in her kids that she forgot about her husband...*

So even though I didn't think much about marriage, I did always fantasize about being in love, and having somebody to be good to me. I knew I would be good to them, and I would think, *I am never going to drop the ball on this thing or that.* I had my ideas of what I wanted to do and what I did not want to do in a relationship. I understood that marriage is work and if you're not willing to put in the work, then you shouldn't get married; just let go of the whole fairy-tale wedding thing 'cause after the wedding is over that's when you're gonna be tried and tested. These are just things I knew.

KENDALL

I think one misconception that occurs is that some people try to group romance with sex. Being married has taught me that romance is a department all on its own. I no longer see it as necessarily a prerequisite to sex. Romance is a lifestyle; great sex is the by-product.

Too often, men—because we are visual, we are lustful—wait until we're between the sheets to express our love for our partner. The bedroom should be the final curtain call. Like the end of a movie, it should be when you roll the credits, and you start to acknowledge her and everything that played a role in making your relationship impactful.

FANTASIA

I think a lot of people have arguments because most women believe that, but lots of men do not. Sometimes women start arguing, or being like, "Where is the romance?" "You do not court me," or whatever. But men can be quick to be like, "I put it down last night."

Or I painted the house, or I cut the grass, or I cleaned out the basement.

I think a lot of arguments start because so many men are like, "The sex is good. What more do you want?" There's a lot more to romance than what takes place in the bedroom. Some women are like, "I do not even want to lie with him tonight because that is all he wants to do. He does not want to do anything romantically."

KENDALL

I get it. Just because you physically hit the spot does not mean you emotionally hit the mark. You come out to play; you swing; you hit a home run, so on and so forth, in the bedroom, but that does not mean the crowd is going crazy inside her heart and soul.

Romance comes in many forms. It is not always in a flower. It is not always physical. Romance can be silent sometimes. It can be simply holding her hand. Or, for example, my wife is not allowed to carry anything around me but her purse. I carry everything; I open all doors.

FANTASIA

When we are getting groceries out of the truck, I am like, "Babe, I can help." But he always says, "I know you can, but you are going in the house." We both know that I'm perfectly capable of carrying a bag. But I appreciate that he's being chivalrous toward me as a sign that he loves me, he cares for me.

KENDALL

One thing I failed to do for probably the first four or five years of our marriage was just to really hear her out. Now, I do not cut her off anymore, I respond and demonstrate based on what she said. That does something for her that hits her like romance. Today, I also understand that simply listening can be romance. A phone call can be romantic. So can rubbing your wife's feet, or coming in and cleaning up so she can sleep. Or it's her cooking for me when I know she's tired; it's her getting something done so I can focus on work.

None of these things have anything to do with extravagance. But many people get married and basically say, "Where's the bottle, where's the champagne?" as though they expect an à la carte setup. Marriage is BYO—bring your own beer, bring your own liquor, bring your own caviar. You're supposed to come together and build what you have. So, before we interrogate each other we must first look within and ask, *What did I bring to the party?*

FANTASIA

The crazy thing is that Ken and I did not start off like this. We learned through our many arguments when we first got together that I had to let him know what I like. Every time he would bring me flowers, he would see me light up. I love flowers. I also love cards—the way Ken takes a card and remixes it. He customizes it. He goes in and writes out his stuff just for me. I have every last one he has given me. Now Kendall and I have learned enough about each other that we are like, "Let's eat breakfast together"; or, "Let's walk in the park"; or, "Let's go do something together."

KENDALL

The reason why men fall short at times is that we do not need what our partner needs. The mistake many men make is that we love through our own eyes. That is not love. That is selfishness disguised as love. Love is completely selfless. It is giving and expecting nothing in return. It is serving. It is surrendering. It is pouring out. You like watching football, but she may not like watching football. How do you adjust? Lots of guys just don't know what their partner needs. We are not accountable for what we do not know. Maybe we are trying to give what we think we like, what we have seen somebody else do, but that may not be what our partner needs.

FANTASIA

You have to observe your partner and study her. Watch her. Watch her patterns. Watch how she acts when you give her certain things, and then start mastering that. I like to go just sit at the spa. Ken sacrifices and takes time out to go to the spa with me. I think he likes it now because it is good for both of us, mentally and physically. He learned to do this by studying me.

KENDALL

If you are going to spend your life with somebody, you have to master who they are. If you don't, you are wasting their time and your time, and therefore, you are holding them hostage. I study my wife because she is my soul mate. I study every move, every mood, and everything about her so that I can serve her and put her in a place where she feels secure. What are the chances that she walks into this house with a new pair of lashes, a new earring, a new nail color, anything new, and I do not notice it? What are the chances that she slides into a pair of shoes and I am like, "Oh, I have never seen those." I never want to be the type of husband who can find every discrepancy on a balance sheet but overlook all of the noticeable changes taking place in my queen.

FANTASIA

I can't get anything past my king. And I love that!

KENDALL

I've learned that keeping the spice in my relationship is an all-day thing. I am crazy about my wife. If she happens to wink at me and give me a smile, I am like, "That is a beautiful smile you got there, buddy." We are a very touchy-feely couple. I am always loving her; I am always complimenting her.

Romance is not always about something that is going to directly benefit you. I have learned, over time, that anything that benefits my wife, benefits me. So, I don't do nice things thinking, *Oh, now I am getting…* That is not my angle. My angle is just making sure that she is straight. The look in her eye lets me know that she is like, "That was thoughtful."

But most men are not raised from youth to be romantic. We are taught to conquer, build, take over, dominate, add a notch on the belt. Romance is a foreign language to many of us. I never saw my mom be romanced. I never saw any man romance a woman. In fact, a lot of young Black men were not taught how to court, how to get dressed up to take a woman somewhere. To say, "The bill will be a little pricey, but I am going to work and save up; we are going. You can order whatever you like. You can get that steak and lobster." So, I always get excited when I see other Black kings and queens walking into a nice restaurant, looking all clean, pushing the envelope to do different things. But there comes a point in time when I think many guys know what to do, we know what it takes, but I think we choose to not rise up and reach for the bar of excellence and give our best effort. Or perhaps it takes the right woman to ignite a fire in us to raise the standard that we often suppress in casual dating relationships?

FANTASIA

Well, I think that sometimes when the romance doesn't happen, it is not just on the man; it is on both of you. Sometimes something has happened, where both partners may have said something or done something that hurt the other. You truly have to ask God to help you forgive them. If you do not forgive whatever was said, or whatever was done, there will be no romance. It will not happen. So, you have to forgive, and stop holding your husband or wife, or your boyfriend or girlfriend, hostage for what's past, because that is not fair. Right? Once you forgive him, then you have to begin to forgive yourself. You may have said some things you wish you could take back too. It blocks the romance. It really does. Once you forgive yourself, then you can study your husband or your boyfriend, so that you can see the things they like, and what you can do to make the relationship fun and make it sexy. I think sometimes that it starts with forgiveness.

KENDALL

You can also reach a point where your relationship seems to plateau. It's a lot like how when you are in the gym working out and you've got a routine. You work your chest, back, shoulders, legs. But if you keep doing that same thing in the same way, over time, you won't get any additional results. You'll hit a plateau. Sometimes, we have to stop doing what got us to this point and start to do something new that is going to take us to the next place. A, B, and C may have worked during the first couple of years in a relationship but now your relationship is more mature and it's time to switch things up. You have to shake it up. Like a bodybuilder does, you have to hit different muscle groups. They refer to this as "shocking the muscles." After years of a certain rhythm, you need to shock each other and do something new and unique to rekindle the spark that lit your fire in the first place.

Love is like a muscle. It has to be trained. You have to think outside the box. So, pull your thinking cap out and open yourself up to learning something new. Study your partner and ask God to give you clues on how to make her feel loved. Do not look at your homeboy's relationship. Do not look at what your father did. Do not look at what your mother did. Please do not do that. You hold in your hand the pen that can rewrite the narrative for your romantic environment.

Setting the Tone

FANTASIA

From a wailing sax, to a peaceful violin—and whether you're at home, out on the water, or in a hotel room—music can play an important role in setting the mood for romance and love. Music is healing and it brings people together all over the world. So why not use it intentionally to create a loving tone in your home or in your marriage or relationship?

As a singer, I can tell you that there's a direct connection between your energy and your intimacy based on the type of music that you play. You know how you walk into a concert and the music makes you feel light—you feel bright purple, pink, yellow, because of all the positive energy in the room? Or how the same band can play a different song that feels very gray and dark? There is energy coming from all those sounds—more than I think people realize.

It seems like no one is singing about love anymore. So many singers are talking about hoes, money, cars, fighting over men—it's degrading. So many songs are like, "Get rid of him, I don't want him." So many women today are displaying more behaviors of aggression than sophistication and composure. It seems like nobody wants to hear a classy, poised love song these days. It's kind of like people want love, but they don't want it, if that makes any sense. Is it that more of us are afraid, or is it that we don't have as many examples to look at? When I was coming up, we had examples. We had the Huxtables, *Family Matters*, *Fresh Prince*. Even the music artists that were out—from Anita Baker to Luther Vandross—they just made you wanna be in love. Do we really have those examples right now?

If we want to have romance in our lives, I think we need to go back and listen to some old songs that maybe we haven't heard before. Play something that may be new to you but back from an era when songs had better messages and people sang about love and working through the challenges in a relationship. Check out some Dinah Washington, Ella Fitzgerald, Luther, Whitney Houston, or Anita.

One of my favorite songs is Aretha Franklin's "Respect." She was singing to a man, "I know you're doing something you don't have any business doing, but you gonna respect me." Even when the relationships weren't going how the singer wanted, the songs from back then were more about trying harder and fighting for your relationship.

KENDALL

I already shared that my wife introduced me to more mood music and meditative music. Calm music and jazz—we both like jazz—makes our house feel good. When you walk through the kitchen or enter the bedroom and you hear jazz playing, it keeps you walking slow, floating easy. This enhances smooth communication, supports active listening, and encourages a harmony that matches the energy that those sounds are delivering to the subconscious mind.

THE TAYLORS

As you can see, creating romance and keeping the fire burning can take some effort. But once you get the hang of things, thinking of creative ways to keep your romance alive can be fun. These exercises can help you keep the excitement alive or rekindle a flame that may have died down:

- In your journal or on a sheet of paper, make a list: What are your dream dates? Write about those dates and break them down until you understand what it is about them that leaves you feeling in the mood, in love, and inspired. Try to schedule at least a couple of dates that make you feel that way. If they're out of your price range, figure out how you can get that feeling doing something less expensive. Maybe it's not about the expensive concert tickets that you put on your credit card. Maybe it's just the feeling of being out in the crowd, away from the kids, holding hands again, and doing something fun with your boo—that a free street festival or outdoor concert would satisfy.

- Schedule a conversation or write a spicy letter or text to your partner letting them know something romantic you want to do with them.
- Make a playlist of music that puts you in the mood. Share it with your partner or even create it with them.
- Schedule a time to share a sacred moment of unwrapping topics surrounding fears and insecurities. Revealing a wound to someone can be very terrifying, but when handled gently and with care, it produces a level of trust and security that builds equity in the romance department.

CHAPTER 10

LOSE TO WIN

Be Victorious

FANTASIA

I had just finished a busy run of concerts at the Microsoft Theater in L.A., the Borgata in Atlantic City, the MGM National Harbor in Maryland, and the Prudential Center in New Jersey, when word about the coronavirus started trickling in. There started to be more and more rumors about how the virus was spreading. When some of our friends got back from Fashion Week in Italy, they were talking about this really dangerous kind of flu. Then we started to hear stories and see reports on TV about people getting really sick. In the industry, there started to be this rumble about how concerts and shows might be getting canceled.

KENDALL

The stock market started getting really shaky. Then there was that one day in March when Tom Hanks tweeted that he and his wife,

Rita Wilson, had tested positive over in Australia and were sick; the Warriors and the Nets announced that they'd be playing without an audience that night; and the Big 10 said that they would hold March Madness without fans. That seemed just crazy! It was obvious that the coronavirus was no joke. But when the Thunder and Jazz game got canceled and the NBA shut down, that's when we knew something really serious was about to go down. It was like the whole world stopped.

There had been a season in our marriage where everything was about Rock Soul Entertainment. My wife was doing shows every single weekend. There were tours going on back-to-back; there were routed shows on the weekends, TV performances, studio time, the whole nine yards. But in this season, everything came to a halt; the industry flatlined out. Coachella was canceled. The Rolling Stones postponed their summer concert tour. Live Nation shut down their summer music festival. My Queen's shows got canceled: Tinker Field in Orlando; Sweetland Amphitheatre in Georgia; the Wolf Trap in Virginia; a Mother's Day concert in Atlantic City. What was supposed to be a couple of weeks became a couple of months, and then on and on and on. Nobody was doing shows; my speaking engagements went on hold. All of us would have to fall back.

FANTASIA

At first, we just rolled with it. I already told you how I saw it as the break that I had been praying for. But then people started getting really sick to the point that they needed to be hospitalized and were dying. And we learned that because the virus can float in the air, singers were especially in danger. The more people who were hospitalized and passed away, the more I realized how blessed I was that I hadn't been performing or working in the studio in New York or California, where the virus hit hard early on and first started spreading.

Over time, we lost a few people we loved and were grieving like everybody else.

KENDALL

Financially, it was like, "Okay, let me just pause and see what is going to go on out here. We understand how precious, powerful, and fragile money is." It became clear that we would need to demonstrate more financial discipline and deferred gratification.

Every week we began hearing about more and more people close to us who were impacted, who were running out of money, whose livelihoods were being destroyed. They did not make bad decisions. They did not necessarily mishandle their resources, but their lives were pulled out from under them.

Even while we were writing this book, we did not know how soon my wife would get back to the stage and I could resume my speaking engagements. And our wisdom has had to kick in and say, "Just because I can travel and do certain things, it does not mean that I have to."

Like so many other people, we have had to make some very tough financial decisions. But we do not do anything on our own; we wait for God to lead us.

Storms Come

KENDALL

Whether it's health or financial problems COVID has caused, or the school calling home about a problem with your child, or a coworker turning on you, or a tornado, or mold growing in your basement, in this life, you will encounter many forms of opposition and attack. Many times, challenges will be deployed against us individually. But in a marriage, there is no such thing as a separate battle. Because just as we vow to become one, we will also be attacked together. Therefore, we must fight as though we're one and the same. And while given the choice most of us would likely decline to experience any type of negative confrontation, all of us must prepare for war. Because hard times are going to come. We serve a God who states over and over in His Scriptures that it is necessary for us to endure various trials and tribulations. God allows us to go through things so that He can perfect our faith and our character as His children.

Facts.

Now, any fighter knows that the worst thing anyone can face in a battle is to be blindsided with a sucker punch. But from rookies to seasoned vets, people are being blindsided all over God's kingdom. All types of believers are being laid out like they have no power, when in fact God stands ready to war on behalf of all of us. We think the reason this tends to happen is usually quite simple: during our best times we never intentionally prepare for war.

As men and women who have served in the armed services know, training and relentless preparation are part of the fabric of being a soldier. Soldiers drill for war, injury, chaos, and natural disasters and prepare themselves mentally and physically to expect the unexpected. But soldiers shouldn't be the only ones who prepare for the worst; everyone should drill for when hard times come. I think this is especially true for marriages since every union multiplies God's power and authority waiting to be birthed into the earth. So, expect your marriage to stay under constant and heavy attack.

I believe we are witnessing so many relationships and marriages being killed in the heat of battle because so few couples prepare for war in advance. Metaphorically, yellow police tape surrounds a crime scene where so many couples' destinies, purpose, and spiritual callings get killed, leaving their untapped potential and those of their children trapped in coffins ready to be laid six feet under.

And since my wife and I want our marriage to be an intentional standard of a righteous marriage and a source of inspiration to other married couples and people who aspire to be married, we know that we, in particular, must be ready to deal with all kinds of confrontation, opposition, and threats.

FANTASIA

From the time I was a little girl, I've always known the power of prayer. That was something my grandmother and then my mother instilled in us at a young age. I always knew that prayer was my key to getting through any situation, any spiritual warfare.

During my life I have been hit with a lot of attacks. Did I feel it? Of course. Yeah, I felt it. I cried about it. A lot. But the first thing I would do is go to God. That was my first thing. When I was on *Idol*, there was this one bathroom where I spent time on my knees before I sang, before rehearsal, before performances. I want you to know that, especially if God allows you to walk through doors, you got to be ready for war. 'Cause with every door you walk through, there are going to be tests and there are going to be storms. I was nineteen when I won, so even though I was prepared vocally, I was not prepared for the industry; I was not ready. The storms came my way. Yes, it hurts. Oh my God, there were storms! But I would always prepare myself through the Word and through prayer and go in ready for war. That was my thing. God kept me and He is the Keeper. Every time I go back to visit *Idol*, I never forget that bathroom; it's where I gave it to God.

But sometimes, we try to do everything ourselves—at least, there are times when I do. We try to figure it out or do it our own way; that's when we get into trouble. But it's much better if you allow God to handle it. It is also important to practice being a praying couple. When I feel an attack coming on with us as a couple or with our children, I will ask Kendall, "Would you take the oil and pray with me, and anoint me, and cover me, because something is feeling off." Now, sitting here at thirty-six, I am prepared. I am like, "Okay, Kendall, suit up! We're in for a battle!" And I just know this because we are in tune.

KENDALL

A lot of soldiers out there have read Sun Tzu's *The Art of War.* It teaches us that two of the biggest skills of a military strategist are preserving your resources and finding ways to impact your enemy's resources. Your marriage and relationship are no different. You have to be ready. In fact, we strongly suggest that you make a list of at least five external factors that could threaten your marriage or relationship. Your list could include things that threaten your health, your children, work, finances, in-laws or relatives, the economy, and so on. Once listed, discuss plans of action regarding how you can prevent or overcome those threats if they catch you by surprise. Again, the punch you see coming and prepare for stands less of a chance of leveling your marriage than the one you don't see coming.

FANTASIA

Then journal about the steps you can take in advance to keep the threats from undermining your relationship. What conversations do you need to have, what moves do you need to make, what things do you need to plan to protect yourself, your marriage or relationship, and your family?

KENDALL

Faith is a necessary component of your arsenal. You have to have that spiritual component. Other resources include your peace, your ability to remain consistent, your discipline, your self-control, your harmony, your rhythm. I've been asking myself what lessons my wife and I can take away from the COVID pandemic and apply as we move forward. For me, some of the lessons were about quality of life. Because since childhood I had been in survival mode, but once COVID snatched everything away, it forced me to slow down, to reevaluate, to take a deep breath.

FANTASIA

I had that happen with me, too, King. I had been going so hard, I got so caught up in the demands that I wasn't finding things to relax and inspire me enough, whether it was a walk in the park, or soaking in the bathtub, or sitting in the mountains, or writing in my journal by a lake. Just doing things that recharge me. I was losing some of my moments of peace and wasn't doing things that bring inspiration to me. Though I understand that the pandemic was devastating to many, many people, it gave me a moment to catch up with myself.

KENDALL

If your resources—your money or your peace of mind—become depleted or your enemy messes them up, then you become more vulnerable to something outside of your family or relationship coming in and starting to undermine or even destroy it. I approach certain things that are trying to impact my marriage with this mind-set: my Queen and I are one. So now I am looking three-dimensionally at the things outside of our union that have the potential to disrupt our marriage and our rhythm, attacking our peace.

There are ways to set up a defense for yourself. You can monitor what you watch and what you listen to; you can put some parameters and boundaries around certain relationships. Because we know for a fact, somebody, something, somewhere, sometime is going to attack anything that is of God.

At certain times my wife and I can sense that our marriage will come under assault.

FANTASIA

Sometimes we will be sitting on the bed thinking about our kids and say, "We have not had drama in about two good weeks. It has been real quiet; everybody is getting along." For us, that means get ready for war. And this is not to be taken as being at odds with particular individuals, but it's about being prepared to bounce back when certain challenges and energies come to disrupt your need of peace and stability.

KENDALL

I think it's important to shift out of the mentality of reacting and responding and instead start thinking proactively. Meaning, do not wait until something comes to snatch your marriage, relationship, or family before you put your hands up to fight or defend yourself. Long before any attack ever takes place, start going to war in your spiritual closet. You can start by speaking affirmations and creating your environment in the supernatural and natural realms, so that by the time you get hit, God has already surrounded you. I watch Fantasia move and change her daily routines and practices as a part of her warfare to control her environment, protect her energy and vibration— protecting her ability to carry out God's calling to help save and heal lives—which is also a critical part of being ready for war.

FANTASIA

Part of how I prepare for war is by reading. I like certain books that make me say, "Oh, okay, I did not think about it that way." I also like getting advice from other people, learning from others' perspectives about how they went through certain difficult things and how they made it out. Because when you are getting ready for war, anxiety will tear you down. But everyone might not be into reading. It could be puzzles, it could be coloring, it could be sewing clothes or knitting, whatever the case may be. But for me getting into the books and talking to other women helps to prepare me for attacks and helps me get through them.

It's also important for me to surround myself with people who remind me of who I AM. One day, I was getting ready for a party and my makeup artist, Essence, was helping me.

"Essence, I am nervous," I told her. "I just want it to go good."

She looked at me and said, "Girl, you better stop carrying that unnecessarily."

Just her saying that reminded me of who I AM and brought a huge wave of relief over me. "Thanks, Queen," I told her as I took a deep breath. "I needed that quick reminder." Because even though it was just a party, I have been subject to so much scrutiny that there are times when I fight against society's expectation that a celebrity always looks perfect.

KENDALL

So, I salute the fact that in that particular moment, Essence was able to help combat the anxiety that my wife was feeling. She reminded her of who she is—and not in a superficial way. Basically, Essence was saying, "Let's get back to this foundation and makeup and mascara, and keep it pushing. Do not forget who you are."

FANTASIA

Yes, talking to other women and hearing their views helps me out a lot.

Reading books and meditation help. I also watch what I put in my spirit when it comes to movies. Certain things will jump on you, and you will be like, "Why am I carrying this? Why do I feel this way?" So, I have to protect myself from that negative energy. If I am going to watch a movie that I know is scary or deep and disturbing, I will have to tell myself, "It is just a movie. It is just a movie, 'Tasia." Otherwise, I may carry it.

When COVID came, we were not ready for it. My income was shut down. So, I feel like we have to prepare ourselves financially so the next time something like this happens, we are ready. You know what I mean?

KENDALL

I am learning that an important part of warfare includes the character of the men that I have around me—my kin, and my family, and my circle. The fact that everybody has a gun does not make them a soldier. Just because you have some kind of weapon in your hands does not make you fit to be on my front lines—or even behind enemy lines for that matter. It is all about your character.

I have found that it is important to start to prune and dissect certain relationships in your life instead of holding on to them just because they've always been there or out of a false sense of loyalty. So many relationships decay over time, and it does not make sense to try to hold on to a rotten one. If you are trying to manifest things that are not visible to you right now, or you are trying to do something that seems truly impossible, or you are walking by faith—and you mention your goal or dream, they are trying to attack it, they are trying to tear it down, they are trying to water down your level of faith, it's time for some pruning. The season for that relationship is ending.

So, part of warfare is making sure you got the right soldiers and the right circle around you. That is also a part of preparation. Those are the things that you could be doing when times are good, and you do not have any drama. You can ask yourself, "Let me sit back and evaluate my relationship. How are things really? Is this relationship moving?" It is almost like how we go through our closet: "Why do I have certain items in my closet that I know I am never going to wear? Why don't I want to remove them? Why am I trying to hang on to this look even though I have several pieces that do not benefit me and can benefit somebody else?"

We have to purge relationships from time to time. That, to me, is also a part of warfare.

FANTASIA

A fan gave us a plant when we first got married, so it is seven years old now. My mother, she's got a green thumb; I do not. So, every time she comes over, she says, "Look at this plant—you have to clip it or it will not grow." Well, I knew about watering plants, of course, but I did not know that if you don't clip off a part of the plant that has died, that part of the plant will not grow new flowers, or stems, or leaves. I did not know that the dead part will also drain the energy from the rest of the plant and keep it from growing and flowering as much.

Just like a plant, when you have unproductive relationships or generational issues, you've got to start acknowledging those things and clipping those dead parts off. It's important to be woman enough or man enough to deal with that. If you've got a problem that people you love are telling you about, then it is probably something that you need to stop. If three people say it is blue, it is probably blue. You have to try to control your emotions and be like, "I know you did not tell me that to hurt my feelings." Relationships that aren't working, you will be better off if you let them go, too, so the old relationships don't end up blocking your blessing and new relationships can come to life.

Even if you're not in a relationship, it's important to be ready for war. Sometimes people say to us, "I watch you guys on *Taylor Talks*. I want to be in a relationship, but I do not have anyone like that in my life right now."

Even still, get ready for war. As a single person, you still have to protect yourself at all times from things like loneliness, hookups, pornography, affairs, and smoking and drinking too much.

Then, as soon as you find or link up with the person you're praying for, be ready for war. Look out for the ex-girlfriend or the ex-boyfriend, or the person who felt like you hurt them back when. Someone who is still stuck on who you were because they were not with you during your transition time of preparing for your wife or husband. Trust me, people start coming out of the woodwork.

Then there's family. Do not be the one in the family who helps a lot of people, because once you fall in love, they may become jealous: "Oh, she is in love. What is up?" Do you know what I mean? No matter where it's coming from, just prepare yourself to be attacked left and right. I am always just waiting on that moment that somebody tries to find something, to post something, to be like, "Look, see, I told you." That is just how the enemy works. The good thing is I've already put my own stuff out there, so there's not much people can do like that to hurt me.

Kendall and I feel like the more God starts using our *Taylor Talks* or this book, the more we are going to be tested. We are going to be tested and a lot of people reading it are being tested, even while we are writing it. You were tested during COVID; you have been tested in your relationship or marriage; you have been tested with your children; you have been tested with your family; and on your job you are going to be tested. Sometimes you lose. But by now, you know my story. I am a real live walking affirmation.

I know this for a fact: After the storm is over, the sun comes back out. And now that you made it that far, you've got more information, another nugget, a token, a little more wisdom, a little more courage to keep going. When the attack ends, you can be like, "Okay, now I know what I need when that next attack comes. Now it's time to prepare for the next one."

Tune In

FANTASIA

Since your relationship will definitely come under attack, it's important for you to prepare for that.

I thank God that I am a dreamer. So, God always helps me understand what's going on through my dreams, especially when I am under spiritual attack. That is a way God speaks to me. I keep a journal of my dreams and have a book about dreams that helps me understand the symbols. Many times, my dreams tell me what is going on.

But I can also tell when we're gonna be attacked because I watch Ken's moves; I study him. We have been together long enough to where I just pick things up. When you have been placed with your soul mate, you just know when something is wrong. We love each other with the love of God, with the love of Christ, and because of that, we are very in tune.

God will also help you pick up certain things about your teammates. I know when something is wrong with my hairstylist and bestie, Derickus. I know when something is wrong with Essence. Sometimes it can be a problem for me because I am so in tune with people. Sometimes I ask God, "Why do I pick everything up?" But that is just me. I'm like that with anyone I'm close to. That also makes it especially important to have the right people around me.

Now, if you feel like you're being attacked and you cannot figure out what's going on, if you've got a close friend who's in tune with you, listen to them. They may be like, "Friend, I have been watching you for two weeks, and excuse me for overstepping my boundaries, but I have been watching your patterns." Maybe you are quiet, or carrying something, or have been drinking a little more than you usually do. They're asking, "What's wrong, friend?" When that happens, I will always think about what they're saying to me because that friend is picking up something.

So, being ready for war, and having the right husband, and having the right people around you, and having the right business partners all play a part. So you can come to each other and be like, "Yo, something is coming; something is off," and take the steps to protect yourselves.

KENDALL

Because Fantasia and I are so in sync, and because our vibration is on point, for me—being the head of the household and being a leader—when things start to get turbulent, I look for third-party interferences. I look for the outside disturbances that are trying to find a way to penetrate us. It could be something with the in-laws; it could be something in the business; it could be something like COVID. Every disturbance is not always what it seems. When 'Tasia and I are having spats, the issue could seem like it's directly between "him and her," but sometimes it is actually about "us and them."

I am discovering that our marriage is impacted by the decisions, actions, and perspectives of other people. So, I am trying to get better at watching out for those things and protecting us. But I find that I am able do this now only because we have done so much intentional work in our marriage, so much self-evaluation, pruning things, circumcising things out. Now, with so many of those distractions gone, I actually get a chance to stand watch and look outside. Do I see something that threatens our marriage—something dealing with business, the finances, COVID, anything going on in the community? Fantasia and I sense certain things, and we feel that vibration coming. To people outside our marriage, sometimes we may seem standoffish, or like we are trying to be secluded or distant, but really what we are doing is preserving our resources for war.

Because if I let the outside, third-party influences come in and drain me as a man and as a leader, then when we get attacked, I have nothing left to defend my family because I gave my energy to petty nonsense. I gave it my energy; I gave it my time; I gave it my peace; I gave it my comfort; I gave it my schedule. I hate time robbers. When I see my phone ringing with a distraction, I am like, "Yo, you are going to hold me hostage for forty-five minutes that I cannot get back. I am not going to get anything of value out of this conversation and you have not changed since the last time we talked."

No.

I have got a marriage and a family that require my attention and I am trying to defend my time. To have a strong marriage or relationship, we have got to understand and preserve our resources.

Win

FANTASIA

You already know about my highs and my lows. From finding my gift at the age of five, to my father helping me to develop my voice, to helping people get saved and touring with our group the Barrino Family, to making my way to *Idol* as a single mom. Maybe you were one of the sixty-four million people who voted for me. (If so, thank you and big ups!) Maybe you saw me skyrocket to the top of the music charts. Maybe you blessed me and my family by coming to see one of my shows. I pray that my gift and praise to God also blessed you.

But my life hasn't always felt so wonderful. To get here, I've had to overcome many mountains. I've had to fight off the guilt and abandonment that I experienced from becoming a teen mother. I have had to untangle myself from abusive relationships. I have had to fight for what's mine and who's mine. I have spent way too many nights crying on the bathroom floor and waking up there in the morning, wondering if God could still hear my voice.

But I want you to know that God never leaves you on your own. I can see how all those painful losses actually helped me grow closer to God, develop deeper as a human being, as a woman, as a mom, as God's kid. And even though I never imagined getting married, God has transformed me into Kendall's wife. It turns out that sometimes all of these so-called losses actually position us to win.

KENDALL

Back when I was in my late teens and early twenties, I used to bargain with God about why He should let me sell weed. It wasn't that I really wanted to sell drugs; it was just the fact that I didn't know how to live within the confines of the limitations of my felonies. Though I'd started speaking and leading guys in Bible study when I was in jail, I didn't always really trust God. I now realize that what I was truly bargaining for was to maintain some sense of self-control, and that prevented me from being able to fully surrender to my Father.

Then one day a message from minister Dr. Charles Stanley, an older White gentleman whose style of teaching isn't what I was traditionally responsive to, landed a message right between my eyes.

"God is waiting on you," he said. "But you're holding on to that one thing. It's that one thing that you don't wanna let go of. You know what it is."

Those sentences drove me crazy. I knew what he was talking about—drugs. I didn't think I stood any chance of living a respectable life knowing what awaited me back in society with my three felonies. (I didn't realize that in God's eyes, any honorable life is respectable.) I was trying to lean on my own ability to hustle instead of giving that over to Him and saying, "God, I trust You to do whatever You need to do with my felonies and deliver the provision that I need to survive."

But then one day, I went in my cell, hit my knees, and I cried for hours. I fought with God; I wrestled with God; I pleaded my case.

"Okay, I'm not gonna sell no pills, but weed is from the earth," I told Him. "It's gonna be legal soon."

But God was like, "No, give it to Me."

I had to give the small and fearful part of me up to achieve my destiny.

I was terrified, so I wrestled and wrestled. Finally, I said, "Okay, whatever."

Two weeks later I got a letter saying they were going to drop all but one felony: possession of marijuana with the intent to distribute. Instead of seven years in prison, I got six years of probation. In less than five years after that, I had built a multimillion-dollar business. And even though I hadn't been thinking about females at all, God placed a queen along my path. Three weeks later, I got married to my wife. The point of me sharing this is to say that men must learn to surrender to God in full. We tend to hold behind our backs the one thing that we believe makes us a man; we think that without it we are lost, with no confidence in our identity. But when we trust God and lay down our arrogance, pride, and fears, He will replace what is in our hands with something we never thought to ask for, could have never thought possible, or even imagined was waiting on our submission to God through Christ. I was not shown what was awaiting me in order to bait me into surrendering. My faith was demonstrated in laying those things down and submitting to God's will with nothing other than His presence and promise in my hands. And it was that level of blind faith that opened my eyes anew to see the paradise He had waiting for me all along. I want every man and every woman to experience the level of peace, provision, happiness, love, harmony, comfort, and pleasure that can come from only God and God alone. He has been waiting on you, so what are you still waiting for?

THE TAYLORS

We are all about claiming the victory, so we want you to join us by using your imagination and getting started now.

We want you to get yourself a big piece of poster board (white or some beautiful color), a bunch of magazines you like or maybe some you have never read before but that you see on the magazine rack (or at the hairdresser or barbershop) and that inspire you. Take your favorite photographs of you and your family and pictures of some of the people whose lives and values you admire. Gather up some scissors; a glue stick; some drawing pencils or magic markers in the full spectrum of colors; some ribbons and maybe some glitter, or fabric, or other craft items. Now turn on some of your favorite music— music that makes you feel peaceful or maybe some inspirational songs or gospel to inspire you. Next, sit on the floor or at the kitchen table and create a collage that represents your dream life. Do not tell yourself that you are not good enough or that could never happen for you. Do not hate on your own vision. Dream big!

After you finish that, to clear the space for the life of your dreams, list a combination of ten people, activities, possessions, or habits you need to let go of. List them in priority order, then identify the three you are going to get rid of first and the date that you will get rid of them by. Then handle your business. Real talk!

Conclusion

FANTASIA

When we started writing this book, we were seeing a fertility doctor, and with my age they were saying, "You're getting older and it's harder for women to get pregnant." For a while it was, take this pill, take this shot, schedule time to have sex. We reached a point where we were over it. I was tired. We just stopped and said, "If God wants it to happen, it will happen."

Then, lo and behold, during COVID we ended up pregnant. Since my caboose was a little older, as my mother would say, it was a very hard pregnancy. I was very heavy, out of breath all the time, and it placed insane pressure on both my knees that I had just had surgery on before the pandemic. I even ended up with gestational diabetes that required me to take insulin shots daily. I went into preterm labor at twenty-two weeks and Ken had to give me another shot every Friday to help keep our daughter securely inside me.

KENDALL

Then one day in late May, I was doing a video shoot for Salute First. We had just yelled, "Cut!" when my wife FaceTimed me and said, "My water broke." I rushed to go get her and we raced straight to the hospital. That was a Thursday; she remained in labor until that following Sunday, when they all agreed it was time to perform a C-section. As I watched what my wife's body endured as Keziah was being born, I encouraged my wife, kissing on her, praying in her ear, just making sure she felt my presence. And I was also talking to the doctors, looking at everything they'd taken out. "Make sure you put that right back where you found it."

FANTASIA

I had already had one C-section, with Dallas, and let me just say, this one was much harder. I don't remember much, but I do know that I was supposed to be knocked out, but I was present, I was there. I was yelling, and I was screaming, and I was telling them that something wasn't right. I felt everything! So, they pumped me full of so much medicine that I started seeing things in color, almost like a cartoon. I was out of it and didn't even realize the moment when Keziah came out.

KENDALL

I just kind of froze when they took Keziah out. I'm like, "Yo, there she is." Just so little. And then she started crying and everything was just going through my head. I'd been present when my son was born when I was fifteen; however, at that time I was not mature enough to fully embrace the moment. Now I was a grown man; the experience was so different. Now I'm barely holding it together just thinking about it.

After the birth, the doctors asked if I wanted to go to the nursery with my daughter or stay with my wife. I was torn about who to be with—my baby or my wife. They told me, "Your wife will be okay," so I went with Keziah. I just looked at her and I just started crying. I just started crying, crying, crying, crying. And I was just instantly in love with her. At that moment, thinking about everything that I'd been through and everything that we'd gone through to get there, it just cracked something in my heart—a crack that opened something inside of me that I'd never been able to tap into on my own.

FANTASIA

When I came to, I was in recovery, and I wasn't allowed to see Keziah for almost twelve hours. A mother's first instinct is to put her baby in her arms and then go into mother mode. But I could not. I was not able to put her on my breasts or just hold her all night. That was so hard. But when I first saw her, I could see that she looked exactly like Ken! She was seventeen inches tall; four pounds, four ounces—a good size for a preemie born eight weeks early—and with a head full of hair.

I held her chest-to-chest, skin-to-skin. I began doing things she was familiar with, so that she would recognize my smell, my voice. I began to sing to her and play the music that I played for her at night-time while she was still inside of me. She is a fighter just like me, and she is already an overachiever.

KENDALL

But when my wife got discharged from the hospital and Keziah had to stay, my Queen, she just cried. I had to put my armor on. I told myself, *As a man, I'm going to be whatever my ladies need me to be through this season. Whatever they need from me, I'm going to be that.*

Watching my wife go through what she did to bring that little angel into the world, I understand love much better now. I'm having a breakthrough. As a man, I can't move forward with business as usual because now I understand a little bit more of what I didn't even know I'd misunderstood. There's no way that I could leave my wife.

There's no way I could love my wife, or romance my wife, or interact with my wife, in the same way that I did before I witnessed this. It's impossible. It would be a disservice to God's creation and His design.

I'm not the same man that I was—and I'm thankful for that. Now I have an even higher duty to nurture and protect them, along with all of our children and grandchildren.

FANTASIA

Kendall loved me from the jump. We've always loved each other, were crazy about each other back when we met in 2014. But I think, for a man, having that true understanding of a woman comes when you get to see things like he saw during my labor. Because now he can see the full measure of a woman—what we feel, how hard we love and cherish. And that we will put our lives on the line for our family. You know, some women die in childbirth; others don't make it through their child's first year.

It's easier for men to run around and do what they want to do, but it's harder for a woman because when we lie down with a man, our souls join automatically. I think that a lot of men don't get it until they see things like Ken saw when Keziah was birthed, but it's important for a man to cherish a woman and love on her because women are different creatures. We were created from what? The rib of the man. Yet a woman's heart is nothing to be played with. She is like a flower. You have to water flowers so they can grow. You have to be gentle with them. You have to make sure they get enough sunlight. We women need you guys to protect us. And when you do, you get a beautiful flower that blossoms and sparkles.

It was a long path to get here from the little girl with the gift of a singing voice who loved the Lord and saw the power of her songs to bring people to God. From the girl who was raped and thought she was ugly; to the teen mom of my daughter Zion; to the winner of

Idol; to having this dream career. I'm different now from the girl who discovered she was being exploited; who was humiliated by bankruptcy and failed relationships so bad that in one desperate moment she didn't even want to be here; who found new life with her son Dallas. I'm different because God finally led me to the love of my life, Ken Doll, and Treyshaun and our grandkids. I will never forget the moments when I was in deep despair and God sent me angels and prayers pulled me through.

Everyone wants love, but so many of us are afraid and scared of it because we want it to be picture-perfect like in the movies. But the movies don't show you the real stuff. Along the way, I've learned how important it is for us to know our worth as women and know that we're beautiful and perfectly made. I know that it's so important for you to love yourself first so you can find the right guy who can love you. Until a king comes into your life and understands that you are that gentle flower. You just have to protect your own self and be with only men who handle you with care. But women weren't meant to be alone. When you become one with your partner, commit to each other. That's when God can bless the union as one.

KENDALL

I am learning that love is an elite course and that most men don't qualify, including me for most of my life. Along my journey, I've grown from the little boy who longed for his father to the young Black man who was desperately searching for belonging and achievement in the streets. I think about the many times that God spared my life and how I found peace with the Lord on the floor of a jail cell on that day when I turned my life over to Christ.

Along the way, I've discovered that in a marriage or in a relationship, love comes in stages and phases. Passion is like the infant stage, an immature introduction to love. I now understand that through its distractive power lust can be love's pure destruction, even though that's what society encourages men to act on. Instead, it takes time for love to reach a place of arrival. This experience with Keziah has positioned within me a deeper understanding of love, where I hope that maybe I'm halfway there. Now that I have a greater understanding, I can go back and revisit a lot of things about love and about my wife that I thought were true and polish the misunderstandings. Love takes a lot to qualify for. Most men don't understand that.

I think some guys need to be challenged with the thought that if you lay a woman down, it's also your job to help her stand back up on her feet. It takes only your animal instincts to lay her down, to go back and forth with a female physically. But it takes a lot to be a rock and to be emotionally sensitive and communicate and develop a rhythm with her for eternity. To offer a woman something that you may not need or even possess takes a different level of leadership that you have to develop. If you're not ready to do that, then just move on. Because that woman has goals and ambitions; she has a purpose. If you're not going to serve her, then just stay on your own.

But there are many men who are good men, respectful men, loyal men, who are working to sharpen their game, improve their relationships, be better partners, be better dads, perfect their role as husband. The best way I can say it, man, is that Christ so loved the world that He gave Himself for it. He was willing to be crucified even though He had the power to turn the tables. Even those of us who think of ourselves as good men, respectful men, loyal men, even great men, can stand to go back and revisit some areas—where you can still die to self, where you can still give more of yourself for the betterment of your wife and family. Continue to pray for and seek ways of higher levels of selflessness.

The Messiah came to fulfill a law that was lacking because of a scarcity of true love. He came to serve and so we all must get back to serving. No crowns in the castle; no crowns in the crib. I've learned that serving is where you'll find your power source, and humility is the fuel that inspires your mate to treat you excellently as the husband and partner God created you to be.

So, serve your wife; serve your partner; serve your children. Don't get so caught up in your ambitions that you forget to help them accomplish theirs. That's a mark of true leadership. Make sure that your wife and your children feel like they have your support, guidance, and encouragement as they try to accomplish their individual goals and become excellent as well. Weave their individual talents, needs, and expectations into your brand of leadership. Nothing—no business deal or job, no applause for a speech, no amount of money I'm making, no car I drive, no session at the gym—can give me the level of validation I get when I see my contribution bearing fruit in the lives of my wife and children. I'm entranced by their beauty above my own appearance. How my family views me, now that's who I am. I am who I'm trying to be to them. Today, that's how I identify who I am as a man.

A lot of guys ask why they should get married when there are lots of females out there and they don't have to. Because marriage is a divine mirror that helps free us from who we are in our singleness so we can become who God intended us to be. A lot of people use social media as a mirror. They put an image of themselves out there and get a certain level of validation and that's how they begin to identify themselves. Others have titles, positions in organizations, exciting careers, nice paychecks, material possessions. That's fine if it's part of God having His full purpose in your life.

What marriage offers you, if you are willing to look, is a true reflection of yourself. Being locked into marriage, being locked into a covenant with my Queen, my true partner, is not the prison so many men tell us it is. It has not only provided us both with a life raft to safety and freedom, but also has become the springboard of courage that we needed to walk fully into our divine callings.

Marriage has also shown us our flaws. It showed me the fact that I wasn't malleable, and I wasn't willing to move outside of my own schedule and my personal doctrine. I didn't always like what I saw, but as I honor my covenant, He has started to use my wife and children—and circumstances around and between us—to help me move toward the more perfect image of who He created me to be. Together, we're becoming closer and closer to the true image of who God says that we are. There's a peace and a joy and a freedom in that that I'd never experienced before when I was navigating through this life alone.

THE TAYLORS

When we met at the club that first night, no one could have known that three weeks later we would be married and that one day God would bless us with bringing a life into this world.

Now we are seven years into our journey. Seven is a spiritual number of completion. We've completed the first phase of our spiritual union. But in order to get to seven, we had to go through a lot of stuff. We had to pass the lie detector test that exposes countless marriages every single day. To whom much is given, much is required. It's only now that we can see how all the parts of our journey fit together. Why it was so important for us to struggle so hard early on. How it was an essential part of God's plan to prepare us for the life we would bring into the world, filling us with a love for God, for her, for our family, for our marriage, and for our entire blended family that neither of us have experienced before. We don't even look like the same people now. Not just appearance-wise, because we're older, but also in the way we speak, the way we conduct ourselves, the way we respond to the world. Because we acknowledge the divine reflection coming through this divine mirror of marriage, we're getting closer and closer to the true image of who God says that we are.

When we sit in the NICU together, we find ourselves mesmerized and overtaken with love as we look at Keziah in the isolette, so small, with all that hair on her head, her little body working so hard to breathe on her own. We marvel at her tiny fingers and feet, her teeny lips. We pray over her little body all curled up in her diaper, and bond as we touch her and hold her and feed her. In the weeks since she's been born, she has progressed from having so many wires and tubes coming out of her that it was scary to now drinking bottles on her own. The doctors are surprised that she's drinking full bottles considering how premature she was, but it's like she's knocking them down. Most of the time kids her age who are preemies don't know how to drink and breathe at the same time. They can either do one or the other; you have to help them. But Keziah will just stop drinking and take a couple of breaths and go right back to drinking.

This new life is sending our marriage into a new season and a new level. Every day as we walk through the hospital it weighs on our hearts. The fact that God has us in the hospital is intentional. There are babies smaller than ours here. Babies with cancer. Babies with disabilities. So, no matter how tired, how burdened we are, we never bring our frustrations in with us. Instead, we act as intercessors, praying for all the babies and families. We smile, we speak to every person, we pray. We ask God to shine His light so that people say, "I want to know what they're doing"—and find God.

If you had asked us on some of the worst days of our lives whether we thought that one day we would find ourselves in the arms of a partner who loves and cherishes us and has our back this strong, we probably would have said no. When you come from communities like we do, where so many things operate against you that a solid partnership seems impossible—or you are in the hospital with a bullet in your lung, or wrestling with God in a jail cell, or working so hard to pay back a million-dollar tax bill, or wake up in a hospital bed after it all got to be too much—it's pretty hard to imagine yourself with a partner you never dreamed of, in a marriage you never conceived of, and with a family you could only wish for.

That is why we love God so much.

One day at a time, we prayed for His guidance and surrendered to His will and His call on our lives. It hasn't been easy. Our decisions haven't always been popular. Sometimes following God's path for us has come with a price. But at some point, even on our worst days, we have figured out even little ways to trust in God and give our lives over to Him—whether by fasting and practicing spiritual discipline, humbling ourselves and setting aside our egos, trying to overcome our generational curses, working hard to learn how to communicate well with each other, doing the best we can by all of our children, or protecting our marriage from the challenges of life.

The journey has been hard, but it's been worth it. One day at a time, our lives have gotten better and better. And today, we each find ourselves with the partner that only God could have sent us, with the family that He created especially for us, and experiencing more and more moments of the peace of God that surpasses all understanding (see Phil. 4:7). We wonder where we would be if we had gotten our way with all the worldly behaviors we sometimes tried to hold on to, or if we hadn't listened to God. Sometimes when we look at our lives today, we do not even recognize the lives God has opened up to us.

When Moses had to lead the Israelites over the Red Sea and then Joshua led them over the Jordan River, God told Joshua that He wanted the Israelites to set up twelve stones as a memorial for what He'd brought them through (see Joshua chap. 4). Keziah represents our twelve stones. She's our memorial to our lives before we could see.

We will always be able to look back on her and remember our days of bondage and struggle back in our spiritual Egypt, as well as the potential as we cross over into our Promised Land.

As the Scriptures promise, we are living life and living it more abundantly. He has opened up the windows of heaven and continues to pour out His blessings.

And in Keziah, we now have a new inspiration to invite you into the conversation about relationships and marriage in our *Taylor Talks* marriage ministry.

God has a promise for your life. He created you with a specific spiritual destiny. And He also created a parter who is custom-made with tailored specifications and who is equipped to walk alongside you in the spirit of love, unity, and harmony. If you are willing to walk through the doors of marriage—as HE designed it—He promises you victory.

Yes, God is waiting on you.

You are going to experience tests and there are going to be storms. But if you arm yourself with the Word, go to Him in prayer, prepare your resources, and move forward ready for battle, we know that you'll reach the unique Promised Land that He has designed for you individually, and for your relationship or marriage.

We invite you to stay in the conversation with us as we grow individually, as a couple, as a family, and as a community of God's kids who are ready to roll up our sleeves to fight to inspire people, save souls, and have healthy relationships, marriages, families, and communities.

Acknowledgments

FANTASIA AND KENDALL

We'd like to acknowledge:

God for being a trusted example of what pure love looks and feels like.

Each other for teaching that true forgiveness and understanding have no limitations.

Our children for being a perfect extraction and manifestation of the best parts of us.

And every single woman and man who's encouraged us to continue standing firm as a God-fearing husband and wife.

We also want to thank our agent, Tom Flannery; our writer, Hilary Beard; our editor, Beth Adams; and the entire team at Hachette Book Group for helping us to share our faith as well as our beliefs in love, marriage, and family in such a powerful way.

ACKNOWLEDGMENTS

HILARY

I am grateful for God's grace and everyday miracles, including introducing me to the Taylors. Thank you, Ken and Fantasia, for trusting me to support you in birthing this dream. It's been a joy, especially during such a special moment in your family. I'm also thankful for Beth and the folks at Hachette; Jennifer Lyons; and Noel, my extended family and friends, and my Enon church family.

About the Authors

Fantasia Taylor née Barrino was the winner of the third season of *American Idol* in 2004, when she was just nineteen years old. Her first single, "I Believe," debuted at number one on the Billboard 100. It was the top-selling single of 2004 and went on to be certified double-platinum. Since then, Fantasia has released six albums; sold over three million records; won a Grammy, three NAACP Image Awards, and two ASCAP Awards; and had twelve top 10 hits on the Billboard Adult R & B charts. Her debut album, *Free Yourself*, went on to be certified platinum by the RIAA and earned Fantasia three Grammy nominations in 2006. In 2007, she played the part of Celie in the Broadway musical *The Color Purple*, and won the Theatre World Award for that performance. In 2014, she returned to Broadway in the musical *After Midnight* and was inducted into the North Carolina Music Hall of Fame. Her most recent album, *Sketchbook*, was released in 2019.

Kendall Taylor is the founder of Salute First, a leadership and training academy. Kendall and Fantasia live in Charlotte, North Carolina.

You can keep up with us at FantasiaOfficial.com, and find our *Taylor Talks* on Tuesday evenings at 8:00 p.m. EST on Facebook and Instagram.

Fantasia FB: https://www.facebook.com/Fantasia
Kendall FB: https://www.facebook.com/Salute1st/
Fantasia IG: https://www.instagram.com/tasiasword/
Kendall IG: https://www.instagram.com/salute1st/